COURAGEOUS UNIVERSALITY

Program in Judaic Studies
Brown University
BROWN JUDAIC STUDIES
Edited by
Shaye J. D. Cohen, Wendell S. Dietrich,
Ernest S. Frerichs, Calvin Goldscheider, David Hirsch, Alan Zuckerman

Project Editors (Projects)

Lenn Evan Goodman, University of Hawaii (Studies in Medieval Judaism)
David Hayes, Coe College (Studia Philonica)

Number 245
COURAGEOUS UNIVERSALITY
The Work of
Schmuel Hugo Bergman

by
William Kluback

COURAGEOUS UNIVERSALITY
The Work of
Schmuel Hugo Bergman

by

William Kluback

Scholars Press
Atlanta, Georgia

COURAGEOUS UNIVERSALITY
The Works of
Schmuel Hugo Bergman

© 1992
Brown University

Library of Congress Cataloging-in-Publication Data

Kluback, William.
    Courageous universality : the work of Schmuel Hugo Bergman / by
William Kluback.
    p. cm. — (Brown Judaic studies ; no. 245)
    Includes bibliographical references and index.
    ISBN 1-55540-693-9
    1. Bergman, Samuel Hugo, 1883-1975. I. Title. II. Series.
B5059.B474K58   1992
181'.06—dc20   92-1757
                                                        CIP

Printed in the United States of America
on acid-free paper

Dedicated to My Dear Friend

Marcel Régnier, S.J.

Contents

Foreword ix
Preface iv
Introduction 1
1. A Philosophy of Courage 7
2. Two Faiths 21
3. A Friendship of Decades 35
4. Members of the Community of Israel 49
5. Cosmic Faith 65
6. Messianic Faith 81
7. Faith and Parable 95
8. Friendship of Great Men 107
9. From Theory to Practice 115
10. A Spiritual Encounter 125
11. Faith in the Absence of Conclusions 135
Inconclusive Conclusions 149
Index 157

Foreword

This new book of Professor William Kluback introduces Schmuel Hugo Bergman, a Jewish philosopher who was less known in the intellectual world outside Israel than Martin Buber, his colleague and close friend. However, in Israel Bergman exerted a very profound impact on almost all his contemporaries in the domain of philosophy, much more than Buber or any other scholar at the time. Bergman was born in Prague in 1883 and died in Jerusalem in 1975. During his student days he joined the Zionist movement. Before World War I, he became acquainted with Martin Buber who was already quite famous. This was the beginning of a lifelong and influential friendship. In 1920 Bergman emigrated to Palestine and served as the first director of the newly established National and University Library. After the foundation of the Hebrew University in Jerusalem he became one of its lecturers in philosophy, and from 1935 to 1938 served as the first rector of the university. In 1920, shortly after his arrival in Palestine, he also took part in the foundation of the *Histadruth* (the Labor organization) and was elected a member of its executive council. Although Bergman's scholarly activity focused on general and Jewish philosophy, he never ceased to take an active part in public life, particularly in the efforts to promote Jewish-Arabic rapprochement. He was one of the chief spokesmen of "Berit-Shalom," a small group of intellectuals and academicians in the twenties and the thirties who fought for the idea of Jewish-Arabic bi-nationality.

Bergman's main sources and fields of philosophical interest were in science and religion. In the first field where he was influenced, among others, by Franz Brentano, Hermann Cohen and Ernst Cassirer, he published works on Immanuel Kant, Solomon Maimon, systematical introductions to logic and epistemology, and wrote on various subjects of philosophy and science. In the second field which gradually overshadowed his later work, he was inspired once again by H. Cohen but this time by his religious and Jewish writings, by Rudolf Steiner,

Martin Buber, Franz Rosenzweig and several Christian writers as well as the Indian philosopher Sri Aurobindo. This part of Bergman's philosophical work constitutes the main bulk of W. Kluback's inquiry into his thought in the present book. Bergman considered these two fields as intertwined and would not have suggested any division between the two. Nevertheless, his religious writings were very different from his scientific inquiries; there he stressed the dialogical nature of the "meeting" between man and God and called attention to prayer as its most authentic expression. At the same time he also emphasized the dialogical relationship between man and his fellow men. This dialogical dimension in Bergman's thought receives an eloquent assessment in Kluback's book which investigates his stance in regard to the thought of various religious philosophers with many of whom Bergman maintained friendly and intimate relations.

Although in his later years Bergman became more prone to traditional forms of Jewish religious worship, he never made any concessions in regard to his ethical and humanistic convictions. Although he admired, e.g., Soren Kierkegaard as the precursor of dialogical philosophy (half of his book on *The Dialogical Philosophy* was devoted to Kierkegaard), he did not accept his subordination of ethics to religion. He rejected uncompromisingly, on several occasions, the latter's so-called "teleological suspension of the ethical," and stated unequivocally that no divine command can annul the immorality of an undeniably immoral act. If a religious commandment, even from God, e.g., the biblical story of the *Aquedah*, the Binding of Isaac, which served as a paradigm for Kierkegaard's claim, clashes with a moral principle, it is the latter which must be awarded absolute preference. On no account should ethics be surrendered to religion. But for the same reason religion ought never be subservient to other, e.g., political, interests, or strive to enhance its own power by political maneuvering. In 1970, five years before his death, Bergman published a small manifesto where he stated his position on these matters very clearly:

> I regard the liaison between religion and politics as a great disaster, a great disaster to the State of Israel and a great disaster to the religion of Israel. The fact that for political considerations, coaliton-motives, etc., one aspires (or agrees) to award political-administrative positions or functions in the state to religious groups, must necessarily lead to a split inside the nation. This evolution which becomes ever stronger in our country during these last months, constitutes a dangerous threat to Judaism and to our state.[1]

---

[1] *Petahim* 12, Jerusalem, 1970, reprinted in: S.H. Bergman: *Bamish'ol*, Tel-Aviv: Am Oved, 1976, p. 52.

Bergman's religious thought was shaped by the above-mentioned modern philosophers, but it drew, of course, much of its emotional content and inspiration from the ancient Scriptures of Judaism. On the whole, Bergman's philosophy may be summed up as a "Believing Humanism."

This is also the guiding principle of W. Kluback's inquiry into Bergman's thought in this book; he analyzes Bergman's dialogue with some prominent religious humanist thinkers of his time. Kluback is indeed well adapted to this task, not only for having been Bergman's student but because his philosophical fields of interest are very much akin to those of his venerated teacher. He has published several books on the religious aspects of H. Cohen's philosophy,[2] written abundantly on Ernst Cassirer, Gerhard Krueger, Eric Weil and several Christian theologians; he has translated and edited Luis de Leon's *The Names of Christ* of the sixteenth century as well as a volume of essays by Eric Weil[3] with whom he had kept up an intimate friendship until the latter's death. Like Bergman, W. Kluback distinguishes himself by his intellectual scope and broadmindedness; although he is not an observant Jew, he is very conscious of his Jewish roots and ties, but at the same time also displays much sympathetic interest in the work of certain Christian, mostly Catholic, thinkers, without sharing their theological beliefs. Bergman, however, keeps a special and preferential place in Kluback's thought. The personal bond leaves a salient imprint on his loving treatment of Bergman's dialogue with contemporary thinkers.

Kluback's expressed aim in this book is to elaborate the evolution of Bergman's religious thought. He therefore does not deal with his many writings on logic and epistemology, nor with his books on Kant and Maimon or the four volumes of his *History of Modern Philosophy*. (Two of them were published posthumously.) His book is an expedition into Bergman's encounters with philosophers who were influential or relevant to his religious outlook. They include thinkers who at first sight appear to be beyond philosophy as, e.g., Franz Kafka and Albert Einstein both of whom were friends of Bergman. Kafka had been his classmate at school, and with Einstein he started a lifelong friendship during the latter's stay at Prague University from 1910 to 1912.

---

[2]William Kluback: *Hermann Cohen: The Challenge of a Religion of Reason*, Scholars Press and Brown University, 1984. *The Idea of Humanity, Hermann Cohen's Legacy to Philosophy and Theology*, University Press of America, 1987.

[3]Luis de Leon: *The Names of Christ*, translation and introduction by Manuel Duran and William Kluback, The Paulist Press, 1984. Eric Weil: *Valuing the Humanities*, Essays, edited and with an introduction by William Kluback, Historians Press, 1989.

In addition to Hermann Cohen, Martin Buber, Franz Rosenzweig and Rudolf Steiner, the chief religious philosophers who influenced Bergman, special attention must be given to the Indian philosopher Sri Aurobindo, the Jewish Rabbi and Kabbalist Abraham Isaac Kook (the first chief rabbi of Palestine) and the French Jesuit philosopher and anthropologist Pierre Teilhard de Chardin. They also formed a forceful source of inspiration for Bergman's religious philosophy. Kluback gives due attention to all three of them, and in particular to their influence on Bergman's thought. There is, however, a certain distinction. All the three were broadminded religious thinkers, but Rabbi Kook and Teilhard de Chardin were nevertheless marked by their Jewish or Christian predisposition. Each one of them believed his religion to be the only true one. Aurobindo, unlike them, professed genuine openness to other faiths and beliefs, according them full equality to his own. While the first two thinkers demonstrated tolerance, Aurobindo advocated freedom of thought. Kluback was also alert to this distinction between them.[4] This explains why Bergman felt himself undoubtedly closer to the Indian philosopher than to the two others although one of them was his co-religionist. This affinity between Bergman and Aurobindo comes to its striking expression in some of his later essays.[5]

Bergman was very fond of the strange term *"believing science"* which *prima facie* appears to be a *contradictio-in-adjecto;* he employed it for the first time in order to characterize the philosophy of F. Rosenzweig but afterwards also used it to designate his own philosophical outlook. When he named one of his books *Thinkers and Believers*[6] this expressed very adequately his approach to philosophy, and at the same time sums up the characteristic features of his personality. As Kluback pointed out very adroitly elsewhere: Deeply believing as a philosopher, he was deeply philosophical in his belief; in him belief and thought were one.[7]

The connecting link between Bergman the teacher and Kluback his disciple is undoubtedly their devotion to the idea of humanity. (This was the title of Kluback's book on H. Cohen, see above.) This idea forms the "purple thread," leading from Plato, to Kant and Cohen and from them to Bergman and Kluback. Cohen and Bergman were a source of inspiration as well as a challenge to Kluback, allowing him to form a discussion of the various modern philosophers who are treated in this

---

[4] W. Kluback, ch. 5, p. 2.
[5] S.H. Bergman: *Hogim uma'aminim (Thinkers and Believers);* Tel-Aviv: Dwir, 1959. *Anashim underahim (Men and Ways, Philosophical Essay),* Jerusalem: Bialik Institute, 1967.
[6] *Ibid.*
[7] William Kluback: *My Teacher in Israel: Samuel Hugo Bergman,* p. 11, unpublished.

volume. Kluback presupposes that thinking, willing, and morality are interrelated. Thought reflects the infinite potential of knowledge while the will mirrors the ongoing significance of the moral imperative. As long as philosophy and theology are founded on rational and coherent thought, they keep alive the idea of humanity. As Kluback stated in his *The Idea of Humanity*, the calamity of twentieth century thought was the deplorable fact that many philosophers and theologians have very often forsaken this fundamental lesson which H. Cohen bequeathed to philosophy and theology of our times, and which Bergman professed in his writings. Therefore, Kluback wishes to infer from Bergman's encounters with contemporary thinkers the following concluding judgment: It is now the assignment of philosophers and of theologians to restore the idea of humanity to the foreground of their philosophical deliberations.

Ze`ev Levy

Preface

This book is not intended as a biography. The latter will some day be written. I have attempted to deal with the ideas and ideals that formed and constructed the life of Schmuel Hugo Bergman. Thirty-two years ago, I went to Jerusalem to study with him the philosophy of Hermann Cohen. I knew that it was with Bergman, and in Jerusalem, that I should do my work. I was right. I found a rare and unique man in Bergman, a man whose insatiable search for truth embraced mankind east and west. From the volumes of Sri Aurobindo to those of Rav Kook, to the tomes of Kant and Schelling, the world of thought came to dwell at 51 Ramban Street. I learned to love my teacher and his influence has never left me. It grows with time and I find myself more involved in his thought as the days follow days. I am Hugo Bergman's student. He was more than an academic philosopher; he was a sincere believer in the Jewish tradition. In a peculiar way, his belief in Judaism made him empathic to any human being who honestly believed, whether it be in an historic faith or a philosophic one. My chapters are written from sympathy for a process of thinking I have attempted to emulate. The reader must understand that I do not separate my feeling from my intellect. I cannot do it.

Introduction

Time had been good to Hugo Bergman. Time has not been good to him. He was given a long and fruitful life (1883–1975). He left behind a grand heritage of philosophical translation – Kant's three critiques – a history of philosophy, a vast number of historical studies and two massive volumes of diaries and letters. The latter are worlds of life that will never be repeated. Men and women walked off and on the stage of the history of Palestine and Israel for fifty-five years. Bergman arrived in Palestine in 1920. In these years, a philosopher, a believer and a public figure lived in the same soul. With him there were other great figures whose lives touched his and whom he influenced. There were Martin Buber, Gershom Scholem, Felix Weltsch, Robert Weltsch, Hans Kohn, Ernst Simon, Nathan Rotenstreich. His life in Jerusalem was unique. From his study, ideas and meditations flowed to men and women in all parts of the world, and to his study they came to converse, to interview and to learn. He was not only a sage in Israel, he was a sage for mankind. He learned from his predecessors, from Hermann Cohen, Ernst Cassirer, Franz Rosenzweig, from Franz Brentano, Anton Marty, Bernhard Bolzano, from Nicholus of Cusa, Leibnitz, Kant, Fichte and Schelling. Names are but signs, directions in paths. Bergman followed many paths, those which led to his deepened awareness of Judaism, those which made him sympathetic to the great figures of Christianity, Hinduism, Buddhism, and to every place where he could meet a great spiritual human being. His hunger for learning was insatiable. His limitations were those imposed by nature.

Time has not been good to Hugo Bergman. His works have not been studied and his diaries and letters only incidentally read. Mankind is never ready for philosophy, nor for philosophical life. The philosopher is always estranged from public life, and we need not hope for change. Every great philosopher knows that he is a child of Cassandra, a stranger and pilgrim in an unfinished creation. Men complained that they could not categorize Bergman's thought. He is not definable; he escapes their need for intellectual labels and safe havens. Bergman himself remarked that he is "between the chairs." He loved the world of opposites, contradictions and antinomies. Listening to him speak of a philosopher made you feel as if here dwelt the truth. We had found the final expression, the embrace that brought within it all possibilities. But this was not true. The next moment another world emerged in contrast to the first, and slowly we became convinced that it also embodied truth. At first, the despair was painful, the immediate insecurity difficult to endure and we needed to escape to a promise of permanent and lasting truth. There was, however, something fascinating in these changing perspectives; something fundamentally human and beautiful. We rejected the absolute that drew to itself contradiction, absorbed it and eliminated it. We discovered variety and irreconcilable contrasts. The mind was rich in possibilities; it refused identification and definition. Bergman showed us colors and not color, truths and not truth, experiences and not experience. In the absolute, he pointed to the death of man; in the "coincidence of opposites," he showed the infinite possibilities of thinking and willing. He showed us the awesome powers of the imagination. We were left in awe of man's life.

As early as 1931, Bergman remarked: "I am strongly prejudiced against the dualistic conception and separation of body and soul." There was embodied a dualism an arbitrariness either toward reason or toward physical, political and moral existence. This arbitrariness led to political and moral indifference and finally to the reduction of the individual to the mass of instrumentality we call the State. The struggle of man takes place within the spirit. Ernst Cassirer had written in 1930 an article rejecting the body-soul dualism of the philosopher Max Scheler. Cassirer's conclusions were deeply significant for Bergman. What did Cassirer say? The great struggle within man is the spirit striving against itself. "This internal conflict," Cassirer remarked, "is really its appointed fate, its everlasting, inescapable pathos. The Spirit *is* only, insofar as it turns against itself in this manner; its own unity is thinkable only in such contrariety. Hence, the Spirit is not only – as Scheler defines it – the ascetic of life, not only that which is able to say 'No' to all organic reality; it is the principle which *within itself* may negate itself. And the paradox of its nature consists precisely in the fact that this negation does not destroy it, but first makes it truly what it is. Only in the 'No' with which it confronts itself does the Spirit break through to its own self-affirmation and self-assertion; only in the question which it presents to itself does it become truly itself."[1]

---

[1] "Spirit" and "Life" in *The Philosophy of Ernst Cassirer* (LaSalle, Open Court Publishing Co, 1973), 876.

For Bergman, this was not an epistemological issue which found clarification in a dynamic dialectical process. As such, it is another fascinating study of the formation of concepts and their contradictions. For Bergman, this dynamic process was a lived experience. With Cassirer, we know how deeply this process belonged to his personal convictions; in Bergman, we know not only its reality, but its actuality. Here philosophy was life. From India and the philosopher Sri Aurobindo to Lausanne and the Sufi Schuon, Bergman journeyed to many spiritual lands and times, always able to speak of men and convictions as if they lived together in a "Believing Community," which transcended physical time in the eternal moment in which the flux of events and change disappeared. Through all the changes of national fortune, from the British mandate to an independent Israel, Bergman remained devoted to Israel's special place among the nations of the world. He would never accept Zionism as a secular movement or the idea that the Jews had no more than a right to survive and become like other national states. The correlation between man and God was mirrored in that between God and Israel. Israel's chosenness was both a glory and a burden, a responsibility that should be beyond pride or ambition. The idea of a humanity devoted to the dignity and freedom of the individual was no human invention; it belonged to the "Binding" which Abraham imposed on Isaac, and God upon Israel. This "Binding" is no single mechanical act; no final treaty or agreement. It was a mutual covenant which was to be constantly and openly renewed. The idea of covenant belonged to the Messianic peace which was the future. The future dominated over both the past and the present. The future proclaimed the reality of the idea of mankind and of "Perpetual Peace." The future was not a vague hope, but a living presence; a guarantor of man's final victory over evil.

Bergman knew that every man could only see himself as a single point of view in the Kingdom of Knowledge. "Intelligence is in its essence, a system of many understandings." Agreeing with the thought of J. G. Fichte, Bergman dismissed every hint of dogmatism and every attempt to impose one philosophical system upon another and to proclaim the superiority of one religious path over another. He spoke of a believing humanism and adhered to Augustine's faith that God has created us that we might meet Him. In other words, the believing humanism is rooted in the Covenant between man and God. Bergman believed that "only a metaphysical grasp of man, a humanism that will comprehend man as the image and partner of God, and which will be permeated with the thought and feeling of the unity of mankind – only this can make a Messianic humanity real. We are compelled to see human history, all of human civilization, as the way to this goal, and by this criterion, to evaluate the progress and retreats of humanity."[2]

We read these words and we know that in them are the expressions of a philosopher whose love of the divine-human relationship made it possible to live in and beyond the political and social events of his times. He lived for a hope that hope was embodied in divine revelation. Being aware that "no man can see himself as a totality of knowledge," Bergman lived with the faith that the particular bore within itself sparks of the universal. The particular was the carrier of the universal and it shared this reality with many others who were through the ages brothers in the Believing Community.

The subject matter is vast and intriguing. The thought of Hugo Bergman is scattered and peculiarly coherent. Bergman brought "the idea into court." He was an "agent of the idea," compelled to see it in all its manifestations. We follow him, not like a disciple does his master, but like the seeker does the teacher who shows the way and says: Go, leave the land of your inherited habits and attitudes and seek a new land, the land of the spirit which is revealed by many faiths and by many philosophies. You must journey on many of these, for to live is always being "on the way." Bergman taught us how to be "on the way"; he never told us which is the way. Although he showed us his way, we knew that he didn't want us to follow him. We wanted to learn from him, to find within ourselves the way of the spirit.

This book is dedicated to the spirit that is "on the way" incomplete and open, but yet determined by a Messianic goal, the unity of mankind in the oneness of God. A philosopher is a believer even in his most radical skepticism. Hugo Bergman was a believer in the journey of the spirit and its Messianic goal. His particular faith made it possible for him to be receptive to other faiths. It is difficult for us to observe a philosophy being so open to religious men and to the faiths of other religions. The universality of Bergman's "Believing Community" was a living community. The more and more we read his diaries and letters, the more we become convinced that the community was his dwelling. He had found an eternal moment.

Bergman loved stories. It was for him a way of communication. At the end of a brochure "On Blessings," there is the story of Friar Laurent who lived in the seventeenth century. Bergman related it with a sense of wonder and reverence. "Friar Laurent glanced in winter at a tree that had lost all its leaves, and in his glimpse of the tree – perhaps a tree that was waiting in winter for the quickening power of spring – he visualized

---

[2]*The Quality of Faith, Essays on Judaism and Morality* (Jerusalem, The World Zionist Organization, 1970), 88-89.

the Divine power that was flowing and bringing life to everything. Having seen this vision when he was eighteen years old, he became a changed person. He entered a Carmelite monastery and lived as the cook of the monastery, and the sense of God's nearness never left him, but remained with him all his life. He wrote: 'In the tumult and noise of the kitchen, of its people and its utensils, I am with my God, in such complete tranquility of soul that it is as though I were kneeling before Him in solitary prayer.' It is as if the lips of the Friar-cook were murmuring benedictions increasingly. This is the effect of blessing: the kitchen remains a kitchen, the cook continues with the work but within the kitchen the gates of heaven are open before him."[3]

We explore the many aspects of Bergman's work. We attempt to follow him on many of his journeys, and we struggle to reveal the spirit in the multiplicity of his images, allegories and metaphors. This is the search for the "Believing Community," for that believing humanism which was so precious to him. He was a guardian of the spirit, and observer of its development and changes. We learn from him to recognize the light of receptivity, to listen to tradition, and to hear the voices of the community. "The Heavenly Man" is the beginning of humanity, the source of the idea of mankind. Spiritual movement is always from the future to the present, from the eternal to the temporal and from the universal to the particular. We study a philosopher who was a pilgrim in this world, who showed us what it meant to be "on the way." We discover through him that to be "on the way" is the reality of philosophy, the commitment to the spirit, and the faith in the efficacy of the eternal. We discover through him a fundamental question: How do we lead the finite back to the infinite? With this question, which was originally raised by the philosopher Schelling, we seek to comprehend man's metaphysical destiny and the ultimate relationship between God and man.

I have not written a narrative of either Bergman's life or his ideas and attitudes. I have written what I believe to be his perspectives upon human and divine reality. These perspectives do not have a chronological order. They are a series of visions exploring the philosophy and beliefs of a thinker who was, during his life, perpetually concerned with the universal problem of reason and faith.

---

[3]"On Blessing" (Jerusalem, *Ariel*, November 30, 1972), 10.

1

A Philosophy of Courage

Gershom Scholem remarked that "Hermann Cohen, surely as distinguished a representative of the liberal and nationalistic reinterpretations of the Messianic idea in Judaism as we could find, was driven by his religion of reason into becoming a genuine and unhampered utopian who would have liked to liquidate the restorative factor entirely."[1] No philosopher was more deeply committed to the idea of the future than Cohen. No philosopher saw more deeply the unity of science and morality than did Cohen. His method was that of the *Analogia Entis*. He could say with deep conviction that there is an analogy between the religious and the moral concepts of infinity. The relationship between man and God is infinite. Messianism is directed to the future; it is a judgment upon the past and the present. "The ideality of the Messiah," Cohen said, "his significance as an idea, is shown in the overcoming of the person of the Messiah and in the dissolution of the personal image in the pure notion of time in the concept of the *age*. Time becomes future and only future. Past and present submerge in this time of the future. The return to time is the purest idealization. All existence sinks into insignificance in the presence of the point of view of this idea, and man's existence is preserved and elevated into this being of the future. Thus, the thought of *history* comes into being for human life and for the life of the peoples."[2]

We speak of a Messianic Age; we believe in its reality and we are committed to its realization. From the *fact* that God is the guarantor of his creation, from the *fact* of its goodness, we know that both nature and societal life have meaning and purpose. There is truth that challenges

---

[1] "Toward an Understanding of the Messianic Idea" (1959) in *The Messianic Idea in Judaism*. (New York, Schocken, 1971), 26.
[2] *Religion of Reason out of the Sources of Judaism*. (Frederick Ungar, 1972), 249.

man's truths and is at the same time their foundation. There is ethical truth, that power of separation that demands the validity of myth, mythologies, idols and idolatries. With firm conviction and moral certitude, Cohen expressed his attitude in a way that left little doubt about the certainty of his faith in monotheism. "If monotheism," he stated, "is the only salvation for mankind, then there is no escape from the fact that idol worship and all kinds of magic must be destroyed. Tolerance is a principle that cannot be valid for the origin, setting up, and establishment of monotheism. With regard to this question there can be no oscillating or any mutually conditioned and restrictive recognition of opposites; the being or nonbeing of the moral universe is at stake here. And the moral world is not handed over to the angels, as the talmudic expression has it with regard to the Torah, but is to be instituted by men in their legal maxims and in their criminal courts. Thus, the destruction of magic as well as of idols had to be commanded.... The pride of human reason became man's greatest affliction. Zeus nailed Prometheus to the rock. Reason brought about the schism of man and his God."[3]

These are severe and hard words that can be spoken only by a thinker of great conviction and faith. Cohen was such a thinker, and we learn of the powers of those words from men who studied and heard him in Marburg. We have lived with the gentler and more tolerant sophistic philosophy that endows every opinion with a right and a freedom of expression which Cohen would have surely agreed with, but there is a level of reality on which man the speaker becomes man the listener, where not only discursive reason and attitude have worth, but where divine truth is heard and man is forced to respond to it. It is in these responses that man discovers the radical separation of faith which separates him from his fellow man, turns societies against each other, and shows how deeply the moral divisions can efface the unity of men. Radically aware of these differences, Cohen knew that there could be no compromise with the truth of monotheism, and there could be no science that was not pure science, the pure creation of the infinite possibilities of the mind. The oneness of monotheism is the future, the hope and vision of mankind. From whatever perspective we approach the age of the Messiah, we confront the unique truth that is the monotheistic faith, not simply the singularity of God, but His radical uniqueness, which implies His compatibility with all that exists, and yet He stands in relationship to it.

Cohen's position is utopian. He noted that "he who recognizes the world-historical idea of Messianic mankind as the task of the Jewish people must recognize in Jewish history the signpost of this goal. The

---

[3]*Ibid.*, 233.

A Philosophy of Courage

question cannot be asked whether God could have arranged it differently, or in the future would arrange it differently; rather the course of history itself informs us of the teaching which is contained conceptually in Messianism."[4] We see in Cohen's utopianism the consequences of his Kant interpretations, his stress upon pure thought, pure will, and pure feeling. Translated and transfigured into religious thought, Cohen crystalized his love of reason into his love of God, although he remained attached to the *Idea of God* as the appropriate expression of his love of God. Grasping the intensity of his love, we penetrate the Idea into the *Person of God*. The utopianism of Cohen's commitment allows us to see the infinitesimal principle that lies at the foundation of thinking, the finite-infinite relationship that governs human creativity and is the goodness of the pure will. Analogous to the infinite ground of human activity in thought and will is the divine reality as the infinite revelation of the divine source of human reality. The future reveals the anticipation and preliminary quality of past and present events. "A history of mankind," Cohen observed, "is, within this horizon, impossible. Mankind did not live in any past and did not become alive in the present; only the future can bring about its bright and beautiful form. This form is an idea, not a shadowy image of the beyond."[5] The hope of the future is the guarantor of the tribulations of the present and past. We love God because in Him is the purpose and goal of our individual and collective lives. The promise of Messianic mankind raises our despair to joy, our misfortunes to hope and our inadequacies to a deeper comprehension of their sufficiencies and meanings.

The future stands in opposition to the myths of the past and the mythologies that developed for their explanations. Myths stand in the beginnings of history and the mythologies become the tool for their remembrance. We study the past not only to learn a truthful account of human history, but also to know the mythologies that conditioned and determined this history. The future is a crushing and overwhelming power. It drives men from the past to the future. "The future in opposition to all these myths of the past," Cohen said, "makes another transformation: the 'Day of the Lord' comes to be 'the End of Days.' With this prospect, in the perspective of an infinite plateau of mankind, the notion of man is raised to that of mankind, as the Concept of God is to the 'Lord of the whole Earth' – Everything in the myth remains history in

---

[4]*Ibid.*, 267.
[5]*Ibid.*, 250.

the sense of the past; never and nowhere does history appear as the idea of the future of mankind under the guidance of God."[6]

The radical change from myth to monotheism is not the consequence of a progressive history, of human reason elevating itself from one level of potentiality to another; it is rather the growing awareness of God's presence that challenges and, thus, enhances man's consciousness of God's reality. But it is not man's consciousness which in its autonomy raises itself to this presence; it is God's hidden image in man that is awakened and increased in intensity as the grace of God brings it forth from its obscurity. Man is drawn away from the earth gods, the gods of fate and punishment that claim to rule his life and determine the course it will take. He confronts God in whom the promise of the covenant is embodied, in whom justice and love create the idea of a Messianic humanity. The uniqueness of God's oneness spreads through mankind as the rays of light seek to break through the obscurity in which man has lived, and in which God's image has been hidden. Cohen showed man that only the future reveals the idea of mankind, only the future allows us to envision that Messianism that will prevent us from returning to the old nature gods that structured life in cyclic forms and brought it to the tranquility of the wheel of fate. With this openness of the future, man becomes God's partner in the redemption of the world from the myths and mythologies that hold it captive. The call for a courageous philosophy is identical to a listening to the future as the call to all human activity and a new sense of value and purpose.

The most fruitful insight of Cohen was embodied in the concept of *privation*. Cohen remarked that "we are of the opinion that Democritus and especially Plato intended for the particle and for this concept a meaning which is *entirely different from negation*, which even reaches out beyond the meaning of affirmation, insofar as it intends to bestow a foundation on affirmation.... Thus it is a question not only of warding off negation, but of providing a foundation for the positivity, the affirmation of being. This privation became the infinite judgment."[7] We have now done away with negation and found the fundamental category of thought: *Ursprung*, the originative principle of logical thinking. What does this theoretical discussion mean for our understanding of Messianism? Reason appeared to have revealed the foundation of thinking, but the latter does not control the foundation, but is only a consequence of it. We are therefore faced with an originative principle that reason can describe, but can never know. This reality or principle makes it possible for us to realize that the presence of God is the absence

---

[6]*Ibid.*, 250.
[7]*Ibid.*, 62.

A Philosophy of Courage

of all that is human and that the absence of God is the reality of all that is human. God's absence is the beginning of man's activity. It expresses a deprivation in relationship to God. What man says of God is affirmative in its privation. The expression is always an affirmation. It is privation that is the source of affirmation.

The uniqueness of God is the wonder of monotheism. We confront the mystery with love and faith. It is beyond the imagination to discover the *how* of the presence of this God. But it is this presence that creates Messianic mankind, the presence forms the hopes and promises that God will be "Lord of all the earth." In His presence, the idea of mankind is formed. It takes its history from generation to generation. Its history is already in the presence of God.

There is no doubt that Hermann Cohen remained a fundamental source of Bergman's thought. In the *Diaries*, he appears again and again as a source of meditation. Bergman referred to him not only to interpret a passage of his work, but to see its implications for his own thought. With Bergman's peculiar capacity for listening to the ideas that move in men's souls he, unlike his colleague Buber, never set forth his thought in contradiction to another, like two opponents seeking for a victory. Bergman's critique was always a revelation that was already implied in the other, but perhaps never realized or clearly stated. Bergman found Cohen's discussion of the originative principle of great significance for the understanding of man and his relationship to God. In fact, it is in reading Bergman that we discover the more extensive implications of Cohen's principle. Bergman noted that the essence of Reason is not "a necessary product of biological evolution.... If we are *forced by a chain* of causes to utter this statement or another, then the statement is determined and necessary, but it is not a statement based on reason. Man's reason (and similarly language which distinguishes man as such) cannot be determined causally from realms where it is not to be found. It is a *leap*, it is a new creation. Hermann Cohen put the matter aptly when he quoted from Zechariah, 12:1, 'who stretcheth forth the Heavens and layeth the foundations of the earth and formeth the spirit of man within him.' Against the creation of nature 'the Heavens and the earth' the formation of the 'spirit of man within him' is an entirely new act of creation."[8]

From the perspective of man as a creature of nature and the attempt to comprehend him from the chain of causality, there is much to be learned of the relationship between man and conditions. Although this perspective cannot be arbitrarily set aside, the truth of Zechariah's revelation is embracing and it is from the embracing truth that we face

---

[8]"The Humanism of the Covenant" in *The Quality of Faith*. (Jerusalem, 1970) 68.

the *fact* that man is capable of the undetermined, the undefinable and the unknowable. Man brings forth, in distinction from the beast, a new set of values which proceed not only from what is around him, but also from what comes from above. Man lives not only with physical nourishment, but also with divine food. Man creates in partnership with other men and the linking is not simply a mechanical joining; it is the formation of a new and unique experience. "The binding to the community is a double creation: individuality discovers the nature of dependency; it thus discovers the fulness of the self. The community is not merely an aggregation, a *Gesellschaft*; it is a commonality of spiritual sharing, a mutuality of work and values, a sanctification of creation. It is a *Gemeinschaft*.

Bergman's Messianism was rooted in the idea of community, in the belief that a believing community is homogeneous in its commitment to reason and heterogeneous in its receptivity of a revelatory faith. Through communication men learn the varied form in and through which the spirit is heard. Each man begins in a tradition and thinks through it; each has learned to walk with his religious and philosophical texts and each has learned that the tradition becomes alive through language and interpretation. For each man there is a beginning that remains the source of his existence and the foundation of his experience. Man learns that there are ways that parallel his, or that go in other directions, but if they are paths of faith, they reveal the moment of the divine spirit. We learn not only by traveling our own path, but through what we see and hear from the paths that cross our own. "In order that I may be a man," Bergman observed, "I have to be able to speak with any other man and we should be able to understand one another – something which is only made possible by the fact that our reason is one, that all men are partners in this reason and we are partners in the common undertaking of human civilization which is fundamentally, in spite of its varieties and changes, a single civilization. We are in our root, a single unity."[9] These are not only descriptive words for Bergman, they envision a new form of mankind that stands before us as a categorical imperative, a moral absolute and command whose voice we must heed and obey if we seek that spiritual change in man through which a new mankind can and will emerge.

Philosophy is at times written with a utopian script. Although from the time of the Sophists there has been an opposition to this utopianism, it has remained a fundamental commitment of philosophy. Idealism has struggled against realism as Plato fought the Sophist and metaphysics battled logical positivism. In Bergman, utopianism permeates every

---

[9]*Ibid.*, 69-70.

A Philosophy of Courage

attempt to write the philosophical message, and in his numerous historical studies he was attracted by those thinkers whose ideals were close to his. He was a passionate philosopher because he accepted Plato's words that the philosopher was a lover and love mediated between gods and men; love was procreation in beauty, it brought the infinite to the finite and the finite to the infinite. In love we discovered the language of the divine that makes it possible for men to reveal to each other how varied but unified is language in and through which mortality and immortality find communication and relationship. Bergman observed that "the common reason, the one language, the one humanity with its reason and its language, is and is not. It is in a process of constant coming into being. It has not reached its fulfillment; nevertheless it must necessarily exist in some fashion, for without this existence, unless we were connected through this stream that includes us all, we could not understand or talk to one another."[10] We read a utopian script, but not a fictitious one. The philosopher speaks from a revelation, from an original truth that gives him the power to go beyond immediate observation and analyses. The utopian script was written in the beginning when we were told that in the beginning lay the Logos, the "dowry" which God gave to man and is still giving to him.

We follow Bergman further. He elucidates his images and metaphors in such a way that there emerged from them visions of a Messianic mankind, the formative idea of his thought. Bergman spoke of the great common stream that flowed through all of us, and showed how the latter had its origin in many sources, "and in these sources the great stream is, and yet is not, so the common reason, the one language, the one humanity, is such because it emerges and flows continuously from its source. And from this source it flows through all of us. Generations of men come and go and the same fountainhead does not cease to pour forth and feed us all. In every act of mutual understanding, in every word we speak, the same stream lives on."[11] Monotheism, the radical uniqueness of God, is the unknown beginning from which everything flows, and although the stream moves into many others, the source remains the same and gives a unity to all. But this unity is not within our comprehension. We postulate it, but we don't know it; we think, but we don't define it, we clarify, but don't drive away the ambiguities that force their way into our thought and imagination. The realms into which Bergman led us, draw us away from the exclusively critical and analytical. We are called upon to think with metaphors and images and to explore the power of ideas, to feel the effects of the sublime and the

---

[10]*Ibid.*, 72.
[11]*Ibid.*, 73.

beautiful, and through the wisdom of Diotima, we learn to pass with the powers of love from the mortal to the immortal.

Bergman's analysis continued. He described "humanity as a bridge resting on two great pillars, the past and the future, and when the concepts of ordinary logic do not permit us to express this strange and dynamic existence in which one reason, language and humanity exists and does not exist, we can allow ourselves, perhaps, the use of theological concepts which come to hand and say that humanity is a bridge stretching between the creation and the redemption."[12] The images which Bergman gave us are rich in their imaginative powers but they are not the nourishment for many who prefer the language of definitions and clarification. Again we find conflict which affects the history of the spirit. Against the Plato of the Idea there arose Aristotle, the thinker of classification and analysis, whose tool was the concept and whose analogies were biological and zoological. Bergman knew that there were realms of reality that defied classification and conceptualization, that were created in poetry, and whose language was symbolic and metaphorical. In each realm there is greatness and weakness, but, above all, each demands a unique receptivity which comes not through training but through gift. We speak of a bridge between past and present, from the creation to the continuous redemption which God embodies and man struggles to realize. Between creation and redemption is mankind, a reality that emerges from the image of a primordial oneness, a "heavenly man" and proceeds to the redemption of this image. Mankind is the created community in which the individual finds the quality of his partnership with his fellow man, with nature and with God. This mankind emerges from a common and primordial source which makes it possible for men to communicate and realize foundation from which all communication arises. The unity of mankind remains a difficult problem since we cannot go to the images and metaphors we employ to express a unity we know lies only in God. Bergman remarked that there was no other way of "understanding this reality of a single humanity except by comprehending the unity of mankind as a unity in the process of coming into being, as existing by virtue of the reality of the unity of God. *The reality of God makes possible and sustains the reality of mankind which is a reality in the process of becoming.*"[13]

We must think of a primordial man as either the idea of man or as the absolute man. In this man all men live not simply as individuals, but as communities. In the idea of mankind, the individual finds his worth

---

[12]*Ibid.*, 73.
[13]*Ibid.*, 77.

A Philosophy of Courage

and his purpose. Bergman quoted with concern Kierkegaard's remark that "the single man has infinite business with God, but no business with man."[14] How do we understand Kierkegaard in *Fear and Trembling*, speaking of "the sacred bond binding humanity together"? "What is the sacred bond," Bergman asked, "which man serves in order to stand before God?" What we come to know is the commonality that reason creates among men, the bonds and intimacies that tied man to man. What is significant is the metaphysical foundation that lies at the ground of human history, the divine beginning from which it emerged. We think of reason, of partnership, of community as primordial realities that man discovers through his reason, through the presence of God as the oneness of all life, of the life of the mind, of the will and of feeling. In the unique oneness of God, man through analogy finds the oneness of human life. This was the discovery that Kant made in the greatest of his critiques, *The Critique of Judgment*.

The oneness of God is the utopian element in Bergman's thought. It is a commentary to Cohen's fundamental claim that "mathematics is in no way dependent on the individuality of a nation. Pythagoras and Archimedes continue to remain the eternal guides just in the sense that their propositions remain eternal truths. Monotheism is, therefore, in no way a strange anomaly in light of the way all knowledge develops. Monotheism is entitled to lay claim to what is methodologically valid for all scientific truth. Monotheism claims – that there is *one* God for all peoples, as there is one mathematics for all peoples. In the latter case, the immortal works of mathematics itself influence other peoples at all times, so that the preservation of the nation of its origin is not necessary."[15]

There is a unifying bond that ties Cohen's faith in monotheism to Bergman's utopianism, to his concept of a Messianic mankind and what he called the "Humanism of the Covenant." If we speak of Cohen's *pure* idealism, we are opening its consequences to the Messianic visions and hopes that are already in it. Bergman's unseen community, those who through the ages have been the men of faith, remains the dwelling of that trust in the spirit whose reality is not in the present, but in the future. In this spirit, the future lives as justification of past and present, as the goal whose realization is the unity of God in correlation with man and nature. But are we not dealing with an hypothesis or with an article of faith? Where would be the possibility of discussion if we deny the validity of the hypothesis? There would be no discussion. The foundation of discussion is mutual faith and without this mutuality no discussion is possible.

---

[14]*Ibid.*
[15]*Religion of Reason*, 252.

We agree with Bergman when he said that humanity as "an organic brotherly unity of subjects does not as yet exist, it is not actual, being merely a possibility and a hope. It is not given, it is rather imposed upon us as a goal to be realized."[16] These are the utopian Messianic elements that filled the souls of these philosophers who refused to be bound only by an analysis of reality and a psychological investigation into man's immediate capacities and intuitions. Man escapes these limitations and his visions and dreams cultivate in him realities that make him constantly dissatisfied with the conditions in which he lives. He needs to think of new conditions and new values. The revolutionary spirit that excited the Messianic-utopian soul never turned away from the reality of the Kingdom of Heaven, from living, from its inspirations, knowing that the oneness of God is the foundation and guarantor of the unity of mankind. The philosopher works from love and faith, with imagination and poetry. He has no fear when he is called unscientific, using at times the vocabulary of religion for that of philosophy. He knows that one is as subtle as the other and that the symbolic quality of the one is as powerful as that of the other.

The utopian philosopher is fully aware that he finds in the Messianic religion "the cells of the single future humanity in process." Bergman always wanted us to recognize "those philosophic schools of thought in the East that are driving to quicken the development of mankind towards a higher level of consciousness by spiritual discipline, by yoga and meditation; methods based on their vast experience and their great fund of religious and philosophical wisdom and tradition. In particular, I might mention Sri Aurobindo and his school, in whom the Indian ideal of satya-yoga was merged with the Judaic-Christian ideal of the Kingdom of Heaven into a single soul-endeavor."[17] Here the script is written with the utopianism that was so vital to Bergman.

He called for a courage of thought that transcended personal interests and which was lodged in the struggle for the Idea that was the creation of love.

Bergman shared with Cohen the faith in the power of the Idea and its ability to realize itself in love. *"How is it possible to love an Idea?"* Cohen asked and replied with another question: "How is it possible to love anything but an idea? Does one not love even in the case of sensual love, only the idealized person, only the idea of the person?"[18] Bergman's love was more encompassing than his predecessors'. His love emerged from his extraordinary powers of hearing the spirit in the thinkers he read and

---

[16]"The Humanism of the Covenant," 83.
[17]*Ibid.*, 85.
[18]*Religion of Reason*, 160.

knew. He traveled to India, visited the Ashram of Sri Aurobindo and kept in touch with the activities of the Mother. Visitors came from all parts of the world to visit with him at his home at 51 Ramban Street. One had the immediate feeling that philosophy was not being composed at a desk, but seemed to come and go bearing new messages from various places in the world. Men and women talked and listened to each other in this modest home. Men would gather to study texts of philosophers, to discuss their meaning. All were concerned to learn, to hear and to meditate.

In reference to Judaism, Bergman remarked that "the great advantage of Judaism lies in the fact that it is a concrete national reality and not an abstract faith. Consequently, it is an organic part of humanity, and has a history which is part of the general history of mankind. Its disadvantage and its danger lie in the tension between its universalism and its national particularism – Concepts such as 'Goy' (Gentile), Edom, Amalek entered deeply into the Jewish soul, and our fathers shrunk from the world of the Gentiles, 'a shrinking both of fear and of pain'."[19] Israel shrinks from the world and feels threatened by it, but this is the same Israel that belongs to the world, that bears the originative Idea of the unique oneness of God, that fought idolatry, the destructiveness of human deification, that speaks of justice and the end of poverty and finds ultimate meaning in these Messianic hopes that make it possible for religions to communicate with each other. Often, Bergman called for a courageous philosophy that could bear the demands of utopian thinking, and stand faithfully with a universalism that created both a profound sense of equality and noble differences, and where learning and listening became the foundation of communication and respect.

Bergman's visions came forth in images of a realm of being that could be called a believing humanism and which sought its strength and potentialities from the Covenant formed between man and God. Man has a partnership with God for the redemption of creation, for the sanctification of life that prepares reality for the unity of mankind, and focuses on the Idea of a Messianic humanity from which human history takes its purpose and its goal. We search for the mystery of this Messianic humanity. We know that it is the hope which creates the desire for its realization. It is the cause of our love, and it is this love that draws our mortality towards the immortal, which is the bridge between the divine and the human.

Cohen elaborated this utopian script with another image. He claimed that "every injustice in world history is an accusation against mankind and consequently the misery of the Jews has been at all times a great

---

[19] "The Humanism of the Covenant," 86-87.

rebuke against the other peoples. But from the Messianic point of view, a light of theodicy is cast upon the riddle of world history. Considered from the point of view of eudaemonism, the suffering of the Jews is, to be sure, a misfortune. But the Messianic calling of Israel sheds another light upon its earthly history. "As Israel suffers, according to the prophet, for the pagan worshippers, so Israel to this very day, suffers vicariously for the faults and wrongs which still hinder the realization of monotheism."[20] Theodicy bears witness to man's need to find a scheme in which he gives meaning to history. The Messianic redemption that is personified in Israel, the overcoming of sin through suffering, is another vision and moment in the process in and through which monotheism brings about the unity of mankind. Man's struggle with God is the inexhaustible source of his imagination, of his creative love and faith that comes forth in his fearless battle to find the purpose of his God.

In 1961, in a diary citation, Bergman spoke of the foundations of his faith. He said: "We have no written book that would be a final authority for us. We have the I in us. This peculiar human authority is the voice in me. We must distinguish this voice from the small I. This is the great danger. For the "temptation" to which we are susceptible, interchanging our I with the eternal I we have no remedy and we can, least of all, call upon an authority. The latter transforms faith into something heteronomous. For who gives authority to authority? We have only the hearing of the inner voice and we do everything to strengthen this last authority. The 'weapon,' the hours of learning that we must make into a way of life, serve this last authority. We search everywhere, for something can be found everywhere. From the perspective of faith, it is all the same whether I draw upon great Jewish sources or others. This may make a difference sociologically, historically or politically, since everything has multiple ordered values. God allows himself to be discovered in the holy works of all religions and confessions like those of Santa Teresa, the tales of Rabbi Nachman, the theoretical writings of Steiner or Ouspensky...."[21]

Hidden in these words is the voice of the great thinker who has the courage to say what most men find difficult to hear. We know how deeply he was committed to Judaism and how ardently he practiced and studied, but it was from this center that his soul went out to the world, to the religious faiths he found in other places, in thinkers and men of faith whom he brought into his life and with whom he shared his. Hence the utopianism of his thought comes forth clearly. We witness a philosopher

---

[20]*Religion of Reason*, 268.
[21]*Tagebuecher & Briefe*, Vol. 2, 1947-1975 (Juedischer Verlag, Koenigstein/TS, 1985) 7/10/61.

A Philosophy of Courage

whose insight into the history of philosophical and religious thought was heightened by that undefined and mysterious power of hearing. He learned deeply from the great Jewish thinkers and poets but he also meditated on the books of Leonhard Ragaz, Romano Guardini, Peter Wust, Georg Picht, Sri Aurobindo. He studied Maimon, Schelling, Fichte, Cohen, Buber, Scholem. The list would take us into innumerable realms of human life. He was not a gatherer of quotations or scraps of biographical information; he taught men to search for the paths that we must travel with love and faith to approach God and our fellow man with trust and hope. He sent us forth on the adventure of faith.

What brought man and God into partnership was not a confession of faith or a dependency, but the expression of gratitude, of thankfulness. Man thanks God for the goodness of creation and in this benediction binds himself to a sanctification of physical and spiritual life. We need to realize how dependent we are on divine goodness, that we lease our physical and spiritual land from Him. We live from the blessings that have been given to us. We hear these words in a great text. Bergman cited Bhagavadgita (ch. 3, verse 12): "He who enjoys the gifts vouchsafed him by the gods without returning them to the gods (in the form of sacrifices) is a thief." Bergman continued with a quote from the Talmud (T.B. Barakhot 33b): "If a man enjoys anything of this world without a benediction, it is as though he robbed the Holy One, blessed be He, and the Community of Israel, as it said Who so robbeth his father or his mother, etc.; now his father means none other than the Holy One blessed be He...and his mother is none other than the Community of Israel."[22]

Bergman was not a systematic theologian. He was a philosopher who could repeat with Cusanus words which gave reality to his mature life and grew in depth as he wrote, studied and spoke: "How can man be a human being without God?" The answer to this question concerned Bergman from a multitude of perspectives, but of one thing he was certain; we do not construct religion on the foundations of thought. We realize it in experience. We search in the past and in the present to find men who have experienced faith. With them we form our dialogues, with them we speak from truth to truth. We speak because we do not believe in an absolute religion. Bergman would say that all religions are for him methods and ways to a goal. Each man feels close to the faith of his fathers, but this closeness makes it possible for him not only to be permeated with his own traditions, but to *com-prehend* the love which another has for us. Only from the depths of faith can faith become universally embraced. Bergman had the courage to say in 1945, that he did not believe in the absolute truth of either Judaism or Christianity.

---

[22]"On Blessings," *Ariel*, No. 30, 10.

This brave confession became the source of his universality. He knew that the absolute affirmation of a religion eliminates our will to find our way to that uniqueness which lives in the oneness of God and is beyond that of any religion. Bergman's liberation from the absoluteness of a religion was his way to the oneness of God. The religious task that is in all religions is to confront the bridge that leads from the denial of absolutism, to faith in God's uniqueness. We know that God loves every faith that loves His love. In the faith with which we love God, we find our way to those who love Him with similar faith.

For years, overshadowed in fame by his companions, Martin Buber and Gershom Scholem, Bergman emerges as one of the great thinkers of the future whose message will slowly go forth to the world. His believing humanism proclaims an ecumenism that will be heard as men slowly realize that we need to walk toward the Kingdom of God in our different ways. It is the Kingdom that draws our faith and love, and gives us that purpose and goal for which God created mankind and gave it His breath. We learn from Bergman a truth has been revealed by many men of faith: divine redemption penetrates humanity only to the degree that humanity is prepared to reach out for it, readies itself inwardly for it, and cultivates its receptivity for God's redemption.

Bergman's utopianism comes forth in words that we have already cited, but should be repeated: "I believe in no absolute religion; all religions are, in my eyes, ways to a goal." From these words arose the dimensions of the moral cosmic struggle "for the expansion of the Kingdom of Heaven which is secretly taking place in the heart of every man and in the life of the whole of society." This struggle was Bergman's profoundest image.

2

Two Faiths

In every decade, at any particular time, at unexpected moments and in reaction to events, we feel called upon to think again about the meaning of philosophy and ask ourselves about its validity. Being individuals of our times, knowing that human life and the need to question belong intimately to each other, we feel bound to question again and again the meaning of philosophy. Why, we ask, does philosophy become the object of the question, and we suddenly realize that philosophy itself had its origin in the question, in man's search for the meaning and purpose of existence, for the processes of nature, and the God without whom he finds it difficult to comprehend his life. The great philosophers write fateful books that explore the crises of our spiritual lives. The books become questions; they do violence to our forms of thinking and we awakened to a consciousness that previously had been unknown to us.

Karl Jaspers (1883-1969) published such a book in 1948. He called it *Philosophischer Glaube*. It came forth in English as *The Perennial Scope of Philosophy*. It was a book that had to be written. Three years after the defeat of a monstrous paganism, Jaspers, a refugee from the terror, had to tell the world what it was to be a philosopher, and to think again in freedom. He felt the need to tell mankind what had to be done to ward off such recurrent paganisms. The book belonged to a time of crisis; it was a fateful book. Every such period in time suddenly finds the need for a book. The book was read in Jerusalem by Hugo Bergman, at a time of radical crisis: such a period in time suddenly finds the need for a book. The book was read in Jerusalem by Hugo Bergman at a time of radical crisis: the struggle for the birth of Israel. It was a book of faith in a turmoil of passion and doubt.

The book made a deep impression on Bergman and he expressed his reaction in his *Diaries* under the heading, "Philosophy of Weakness and

Philosophy of Strength." The frightening consequence of nihilism demands that we return to God. No matter how we describe the conditions through which man has lived, what is of vital importance is the message that the philosopher sets before mankind. Bergman believed that the philosopher has a responsibility to speak to all men, to speak of human values and the destiny of mankind. "We are obligated to send forth a message, a powerful vision of what philosophy has to say now." We need "a great vision of the responsibility of the philosophically thinking man confronting an age hidden in utilitarianism, materialism and technology. If Jaspers asks what Tolstoy once so penetratingly asked: 'What should we do?' his voice becomes weaker. He knows what he would like but he knows at the same time that mankind will not go this way. What he would like is the renewal of philosophical faith hidden in religion. He would like the transformation of religion into philosophy. That will certainly not be the way of mankind, even though it might be the way of a few."[1]

If Bergman found Jaspers's intentions similar to his own, he found his answer to the question "What should we do?" to be inadequate. The problem is to find an answer that is more suitable for a mankind that not only needs the understanding of the philosopher, but also a way beyond this understanding, the way that will not only show the significance of a vision, but also the way of its realization. Bergman assumed a responsibility that was awesome and he stated his position twelve years later in an article entitled, "The Need for a Courageous Philosophy."

He began the article with a direct reference to Jaspers's book: "These lines," he said, "are written under the profound impression of Karl Jaspers's little volume, *Philosophischer Glaube*."[2] Bergman was moved by the paradox that he knew confronted the philosopher. There was the profound commitment to reason, faith in its perennial power to reveal man's unconquerable spirituality, his capacities for understanding and his ability to live through the Idea. But there was another reality, the violence that threatened both the understanding and the reason, that rose from man's sensuality, and forged barriers and rejections of any meaningful discussion of the Idea of Mankind. Bergman noted that the book was evocative "by virtue of its faith in philosophy and at the same time, it stirs one with its own weakness and the helplessness of the philosophy which it presents to suffering humanity."[3] A line of the French novelist and literary critic Maurice Blanchot, seems to break the

---

[1] *Tagebuecher & Briefe*, Vol. 2, 2/23/49.
[2] *The Need for a Courageous Philosophy*, in *Scripta Hierosolymitana*, Studies in Philosophy, 1960, Vol. 6, 104.
[3] *Ibid.*

Two Faiths

silence which we feel before this paradox: "As we write the work, we are drawn by the absence of the work."[4] We seek a way that will take us toward that transformation of mankind, that will allow the Idea to become reality, if not at the moment, in the future. We are haunted by the question of "What shall we do?" It is the question that accompanies our dreams and our hopes; it is the question that does violence to our lassitude and pessimism. The question is always there, accompanying the words we write and the actions we achieve. It is the remainder of the absence of the work.

Bergman remarked that Jaspers believed that "the worst thing that could happen to humanity in this time so charged with great responsibilities, would be for the crisis to pass without anything happening to man as man; without his hearing transcendence or having his sight and action clarified. This would indeed cause a terrible loss in the consciousness of man and we would sink."[5] Jaspers realized how deeply philosophy is tied to the "event" that had become a moral and political crisis. The depth of the crisis was monumental and the experience challenged beyond the imaginative powers of man, and yet this crisis had to be spoken of, reintegrated into the history of mankind. The greatest danger would be its loss, the attempt of man to forget what must always be a part of his awareness. Jaspers stated clearly that "the great danger is that what happened may pass, considered as nothing but a great misfortune, without anything happening to us men as men, without hearing the voice of transcendence, without our attaining to any insight and acting with insight. A tremendous decrease in clear awareness would then cause us to sink into a narrowed existence."[6]

Philosophy is often a response to a crisis, to a rupture that has to be overcome. We confront an unknown haunting that causes us to find ways to overcome the separation that is the crisis. The past can no longer be the past, nor the present the present. Karl Jaspers, like Bergman, knew that there was a monumental abyss separating the past from the present, and philosophy confronted by its reality, would confront a radically different task. It would need a new language and questions would follow answers with rapidity and violence.

What is the call of philosophy? "Philosophy," Bergman said, "has to call upon the man of our times, the man who bows before matter and the machine, the man for whom science has become technology instead of wisdom, and whose faith in the 'thing' is liable to swallow him – and

---

[4] "The Absence of the Book" in *The Gaze of Orpheus* (Barrytown Station Hill, 1981), 148.
[5] *The Need for a Courageous Philosophy*, 104.
[6] *The Perennial Scope of Philosophy* (Archon Books, 1968) 169-170.

philosophy has to say to him again and again: The reality and concreteness of the world is merely a reality stretched between the Divine and the Self and has no existence without them."[7]

There is a deep division between Jaspers and Bergman. Bergman is a believer in the immediacy of the divine Presence. Faced with the most immoral situations, the reality of man's moral degeneracy, the irreconcilable hatred of Jew and Arab, he remained confident in the Word of God. Although that trust was deeply questioned, Bergman remained faithful to the tradition in all its ceremonial forms. We feel this trust in a diary entry of 1958, where Bergman spoke of "his prayerful endeavor to meditate about the divine Greatness and the love for God. Both are very difficult. Greatness: whatever man thinks of as great and would like to ascribe to it, is too small. I would like, out of the many books that I read, to have *one* sentence which can be bestowed upon me as the consequence of the day, only *one* sentence."[8]

Bergman struggled in prayer. He struggled like Jacob to gather for himself a blessing. This was the confrontation with the Biblical God who appeared to Moses and sent Abraham forth to a new land and a new historical destiny. Answers and questions flowed from within the tradition. He found Jaspers inadequate. There was no historical tradition in and from which a divine confrontation could take place. Jaspers stood within philosophy but the latter knows no concrete decision to a divine command. There are no Fathers and no Teacher.

Jaspers realized that "if faith is neither solely content nor solely an act of the subject, but is rooted in the vehicle of phenomenality, then it should be conceived only in conjunction with that which is neither subject nor object but both in one, with that which manifests itself in the duality of subject and object."[9] If the being of the world is not being itself, then we can make no final judgment of the world, the world is knowable only as phenomena and as such is capable of unending possibilities of meaning. If the world is not explicable, definable or even comprehensible from and within itself, then the phenomenality of the world can be grasped only by an act of faith. From the perspective of the world, nothing that is said of the world from the presence of God is knowable, but the presence of God, if not knowable, is the consequence of faith and it is from this faith, from this epiphany that the world has purpose and goal. The awareness of the phenomenal nature of the world is an ongoing and perplexing situation for man. From the time of the Sophists to Kant, this reality had been recognized and commented upon.

---

[7]*The Need for a Courageous Philosophy*, 104-105.
[8]*Tagebuecher*, 10/7/58.
[9]*The Perennial Scope of Philosophy*, 9.

Two Faiths 25

The reality of God became less and less assured. Man's dissatisfaction with the limits of his knowledge, forced him to realize that within him there were levels of consciousness that heard and grasped realities that were beyond knowledge and analysis.

Bergman was disturbed by the following remarks made by Jaspers. He believed that if they were accepted, philosophy would yield its reality as a meaningful force in the world, the truth from which all other truths follow. Jaspers stated: "The philosopher cannot possibly tell the theologians and the churches what to do. The philosopher can only hope to help create the preliminary requirements. He would like to help prepare the ground and to help produce awareness of the intellectual situation necessary for the growth of what he himself cannot create." We read these words with the sadness of resignation. The philosopher has grown pale alongside the theologian; philosophical faith is a thin light compared with the richness of religious commitment. Jaspers realized how deep had been the spiritual change in man's situation, a change that was so radical that it demanded a corresponding challenge from our Biblical faith. "Hence," Jaspers continued, "it is in order that we do everything in our power to restore the eternal truth, we must plumb its very depths and, unconcerned over what is transient and historical, utter truth in a new language. Here the philosopher only becomes involved in questions that he cannot answer though he knows that the future will assuredly give the answer."[10]

Bergman believed that these were Jaspers's final words and they reflected "the philosopher's renunciation out of despair." There is an even deeper sadness in Bergman's comments. He is painfully aware that there is a renunciation in Jaspers's words. He noted that philosophy keeps relinquishing and resigning, even though Jaspers says again and again that philosophy should by no means abdicate, especially today. "This is what is so staggering," Bergman observed, "about this little and great volume. Before us we have a philosopher who sees the mortal illness of our time deeply and penetratingly.... He apprehends from where the redemption may come, but at the decisive moment, he declines to give his answer. Why does he refuse? He is afraid, lest by a too clear and distinct word, that which can only be the experience of a moment will turn into a thing...he is afraid of turning God and the Self (or, as he so carefully puts it: Transcendence and existence) into things. He knows, of course, that philosophy can develop and grow only in a people that has a religious faith, but he relinquishes the position and privilege of leadership to the church and the religions, saying, In all philosophizing effort there is a tendency to help the religious

---
[10]*Ibid.*, 109.

institutions. Philosophy affirms them, affirms their existence in the world, without the philosopher being able to take a direct part in them."[11]

Bergman's remarks were serious and painful. We are forced to see our weakness and inadequacy. We feel the bounds of our limitations, the phenomenological quality of our knowledge, but we know that we are beyond these limitations, that truth does not lie within the question about the possibility of knowledge but in another question: How do we know? There are other ways of knowing our vehicles to paths of truth. We cannot allow the skepticism, the fatefulness of our mortality to become the captors of our reality. The nihilism which we know is a common consequence of such skepticism confronting levels of faith that come to man through a wider and deeper understanding of knowledge, a knowledge that emerges from faith. Why, we ask, do we limit knowledge to what can be known in time and space, to what can be structured by the categories of the understanding? Knowledge that is not preceded by faith is skepticism.

We are stunned by the failure of Jaspers's book. Is it the failure of contemporary philosophy to confront the pessimism, materialism, and nihilism of contemporary values with the faith of the divine presence? Is the resignation of philosophy to phenomenology the consequence of its refusal to turn to God, to be a religious philosophy, to find again its identification with revelation that it has lost since the classical and medieval periods? Bergman put forth another question: "Does philosophic belief have to be counterfeit in order to act? Can it not act directly? Whence this weakness? It seems as though the philosophers are afraid and that fear paralyzes them."[12]

What are the fears of the philosophers, the lovers of wisdom, that makes it impossible for them to act only from the "as if" perspective, rather than from the love and hope that faith precedes all doing. These are words to be heard, but these are the words of the religious, of men who have fought with their faith and sought it in the constancy of strength that comes from the *Magisterium*. There is the mystery of which the Jesuit father Yves de Montcheuil spoke: "No doubt mystery will always pose an acute problem for reasoning intelligence; but for another part of the spirit – indeed a part that is superior to the reasoning intelligence – mystery constitutes a fundamental need, a necessary nourishment...a task that has not always been properly developed among Christians. This can be seen from how little the great Christian

---

[11]*The Need for a Courageous Philosophy*, 106-107.
[12]*Ibid.*, 107.

mysteries figure in the things that really motivate and inspire their thought and action."[13]

Bergman knew that philosophy, as the dimensions of critical reason, was not enough. He realized how powerful the latter was as an instrument of analysis, how well it answered our question about the possibilities of knowledge and the limits of the knowing, but philosophy had abandoned to the other arts and sciences realms of reality that philosophy could no longer approach. Instead of being the Queen of the Sciences, she had become one among them. Limited to the phenomenal quality of knowledge, she remained within the limitations. Although she allowed the reason to speculate with aesthetic and rational ideas, there remained only possibilities, the "as if" conditions of human life. For the higher realms of knowledge, for a grasping and deeper exploration of the mystery of the divine incarnation, she retreated as a doctor of ignorant learning. She yielded to the Magisterium of the historical religious discussions of love and hope, and the experience of divinity upon mortality. Suddenly these realms were ruptured from each other and became strange to each other. Philosophers were put on one side, theologians on another, the division of work overtook the human endeavor with fateful consequences. Thinkers had to declare where they stood, and to express their thoughts only in the language of their professions.

If philosophy is to retain its universality, where must it remain, and from which question must it constantly hold forth its discourses and determine its actions? It must again join faith and knowledge. Philosophy has never been legitimately separated from the meaning of man's confrontation with God, from the question of man's essence and from the destiny of the soul. These were the metaphysical questions that gave philosophy its uniqueness, its love of wisdom. Man found in "a dark secret night" his divine redemption, his contemplation of ideas and the tranquility and happiness that is in the laws that govern reality. We have regrets that the limitations of our knowledge do not allow us to prove cosmologically or ontologically the existence of God, but our religious needs are not dependent on the possibilities of knowledge. The wonders of the creation remain beyond proofs; they forge within the imagination of new powers of purpose and meaning. We are overwhelmed by the beauty of order and the sublimity of the majesty that is God. "And if we cannot prove the existence of God in this manner," Bergman remarked, "the wisdom reigning in nature does exist,

---

[13]Yves de Montcheuil 1899-1944, in Henri de Lubac *Three Jesuits Speak* (San Francisco, Ignatius Press, N.D.), 54.

even with all its shortcomings, and it certainly exceeds all the wisdom that is man. That is a fact."[14]

If we discover the limits of our epistemological possibilities, we do not at the same time reveal the inadequacies of the proofs themselves. The ontological proof of God's existence is irrefutable as an act of faith and true as the knowledge of faith, but not true for our knowledge, limited to time and space. Our insufficiencies ought not to be imposed on the reality which is above and prior to us. "Truth," Bergman stated, "is essentially existential and the mutual relationship between truth and existence is expressed in the struggle around the ontological proof.... Truth is fundamentally existential, truth is not a dead mathematical formula written in some book, it is not a shadow among shadows but something living and present, containing in itself the pulsating power of realty."[15]

Bergman is speaking of truth as the living divine. This is a truth that is indefinable, whose powers surpass man's capacity to limit them. Man is aware that what he calls truth is not a faculty that he can control and dominate; it is a force that causes him wonder. He stands in awe of the beauty and sublimity which reveal to him the unimaginable mystery of the divine soul that fills his reality. Man's evolution has been a deeper and deeper exploration of the soul that defies limitation and gives man renewed hope and love, makes it possible for him to defy that pessimism that brings with it moral and political degeneracy. In man's awareness of his epistemological boundaries lies his realization that these are boundaries that are self-imposed, that man can learn to comprehend the presence of a spiritual world which can be heard and grasped. There are levels of meaning which we have not as yet penetrated, but which communicate with us. We follow the paths of science and we wonder at their precision and technological advances, but we wonder more at the spiritual powers that have made these advances possible. The latter do not necessarily bring with them fundamental changes in man's spiritual nature whose powers were the secret of the two great philosophers of antiquity: Plato and Pythagoras. We understand this as we listen to these wonderful words of Plato in the *Phaedo:* "And I fancy that these men who established the mysteries were not unenlightened, but in reality had a hidden meaning when they said long ago, that whoever goes uninitiated and unsanctified to the other world will lie in the mire, but he who arrives there initiated and purified will dwell with the gods. For as they say in the mysteries, the thyrsus-bearers are many but the

---

[14]*The Need for a Courageous Philosophy*, 109-110.
[15]*Ibid.*, 110.

mystics few; and these mystics are, I believe, those who have been true philosophers."[16]

We speak of the revolution that science has accomplished in our lives and will achieve in the future, but the revolution must not be only quantitative, but also qualitative. The ancients understood the radical changes that the philosopher must undergo to be capable of grasping the communication that comes not only from the soul but from what is above the soul. Bergman, who deeply appreciated the *Science et Réalité* (1954) of the philosopher Ferdinand Brunner, reminded us that "modern man is made to feel his superiority to the ancient man who created these rites and rituals, and the rituals are generally seen as a collection of superstitions and childish beliefs. Nevertheless, investigators with a broader horizon are gradually freeing themselves of these superstitions of *our* own times and paving the way to a true understanding of the past."[17]

Bergman opened the way to an understanding of reality that went far beyond mechanical-causal explanations. The more and more we find ourselves embedded in such explanations, the more we realize how deeply we are binding man to a single level of reality. We cut away every dimension of life that is not embraced by the causal structure. In other words, the Ancients are dismissed as harbingers of superstition and creators of mockery. They were lovers of wisdom who believed that only those who were initiated in love could comprehend how this love could bring a man from mortality to divinity, who knew the transformative powers that occur in "the dark night of the soul." Even Socrates had only begun to ask simple questions about the powers of love.

Bergman was convinced that the food of life didn't come solely from the ground, but from above, as Kafka described it in his tale "The Investigations of a Dog." We read about it in the "Allegory of the Cave" in the sixth book of the *Republic*. The light from above and its reception gives a new view of the world about us. Men see differently; they see according to the light that is available to them. The obscurity or brightness of their perception depends upon the openness to what is above them and its communicating power. Bergman referred to the teaching of the *Kabbalah* and its Tree of *Sefirot*. "The *Sefirah* of the *Kingdom* which receives its abundance from the higher *Sefirot* and it, the lowest *Sefirah*, is in this respect the hidden symbol of the revealed Cosmos." To explain this movement from above to the below, he cited the words of Meister Eckhart: "It corresponds to the nature of the above

---

[16]*Phaedo* (Cambridge, Harvard University Press, 1947), 69 C-D.
[17]*The Need for a Courageous Philosophy*, 112.

to have influence essentially upon what is below; on the other hand, it is the nature of the below to receive what comes from the above."[18]

Bergman noted that we have more often desired to explain the world horizontally than vertically, and we have to our detriment sought to eliminate the vertical emanations. This does not mean that we must now substitute one for the other, but it does mean that we must put one alongside the other and attempt to discover how they complement each other. This way of seeing, both vertically and horizontally, became one of the most provocative and original aspects of Bergman's philosophy. He believed that "these upper worlds of the spirit sometimes interfere or break through to the lower worlds and determine the divisions of events without any of us, who are still bound to material considerations, being able to explain the changes."[19]

Bergman did not separate the ascent in evolution from the descent from above. Evolution prepares the ground for revelation. We realize that revelation is dependent upon our ability to receive and we have no way of knowing how and when revelation will occur, but we do know that neither evolution nor revelation is complete without the other. We stand at the beginning of man's confrontation with God. We move towards the future with hope and love. We understand the incompleteness of our reality; we know that we have not found the truth of our being. God has only begun to reveal to us the meaning of our existence. Bergman was fond of quoting from a book called *Consolation of Philosophy* written by a well-known Prague biologist Emmanuel Radl. Radl had fallen sick in 1937 and until his death in 1942, remained in seclusion. The years of seclusion forced him to think often about the meaning of life. He noted in his book ideas that were very precious to Bergman: "I have separated myself," he said, "from the new biological science because it occupies itself only with matter; around it reigns darkness. I hereby return to the method of ancient times and of the Middle Ages. If I want to comprehend living things, I explain the frog by the form of the vertebrae, the ape by man and man himself by God."[20] In other words, it is hardly possible to be a man without God.

In Bergman's attempt to show a new philosophical way, to make us aware of Jaspers's inadequacies, there is no reference to either Judaism or Christianity, or any other historical religion. He doesn't ask us to return to a religious tradition, but he does urge us to consider the more universal problem of man's relationship to God: the interrelation between the ascent from below and the descent from above. Bergman

---

[18]*Ibid.* fn. 5, 114.
[19]*Ibid.*, 114.
[20]*Ibid.*, 116.

Two Faiths

found in Sri Aurobindo, the Indian philosopher, a profound devotion to the idea and he remained deeply influenced by Sri Aurobindo to the end of his life. Bergman was absorbed by this idea and it became one of the fundamental forces of his philosophical life. He put it in the form of a question: "Is it at all possible for man to elucidate things from above, can he raise himself at all to those higher worlds of form, which, as has been said, determine the face of nature and history? Perhaps man has to put up with this horizontal, causal-mechanistic interpretation only because he *cannot* raise himself above the mechanical world revealed to him by the senses. Are there any means at all of ascending to those layers of being which are not revealed to the senses even if they do exist?"[21]

Our world has given much attention to Freud's notion of sublimation, but seems to care little for the purification that was vital to the Pythagoreans, the neo-Platonists and much of the speculative philosophy of India. Sri Aurobindo described this Yoga of self-purification: He said that "the will is perfected when it gets away from and behind its impulses and its customary ruts of effectuation and discovers an inner power of the spirit which is the source of an intuitive and luminous action and an original harmonious creation. The movement of perfection is away from all domination by the lower nature and towards a pure and powerful reflection of the being, power, knowledge and delight of the Spirit and Self in the Buddhi."[22]

Bergman sought a philosophy that would embrace new directions of thought, and that would be open to new worlds of communication as man's purification allows him to become more and more receptive to greater spiritual realities. Philosophy, as Plato described it, is an initiation, a spiritual preparation for spiritual energies, new forms of the imagination, and enhanced capacities of listening and seeing. He preferred to speak as a Jew or offer the insights and wisdom of his own faith. His own spiritual preparation and education was embedded in his tradition and he practiced it with devotion and truthfulness, but he knew that mankind needed to be awakened to the universal awareness of the Divine presence. From this awareness, man would find ways to realize how deeply divinity influences the creation. He repeated often that it was the task of philosophy, art, and religion to show man the way "to live in the *wholeness* of his personality so far as he is able; yet our technological culture narrows and degrades the consciousness of man. It is the duty of philosophy to awaken man to the danger that here threatens him."[23]

---

[21]*Ibid.*, 117.
[22]*The Synthesis of Yoga* (Pondicherry, Sri Aurobindo Ashram, 1988), 642.
[23]*The Need for a Courageous Philosophy*, 118.

Bergman had broken through to states of consciousness that would be skeptically set aside by our pragmatic intelligence. He knew that their objectivity and truth demanded higher forms of intelligence and appreciation and that we were not yet capable of acknowledging their reality. Bergman sought that transformation that Plato had spoken of in the *Phaedo*. We must break through the "shells" that blend and limit the levels of consciousness, that force us back into the cave. The light hurts and blinds our eyes, but it is truth and we must learn to see with it.

Bergman rarely advised his colleagues about their task, but he was willing to say that "the philosopher has to see and understand that consciousness of today is only a small sector of a whole range of possible awareness.... In this way, too, the problem of immortality, the whole question of the life of man before truth and after death, the problem now living in philosophy like a shadow, will take on the depth and vitality which a merely intellectual approach could not possibly give it. The philosopher must strive by himself, as far as he is able, to expand his consciousness beyond the limits of mentality."[24] Where, we ask, was Bergman taking us? What paths did he ask us to follow? We answer with an openness that is rare in the history of thought. He asked us to follow on that path which would lead to a greater awareness of our divine-human destiny, one that is always in confrontation with the presence of God. He asked us to relate that divine outflow which is determined by our powers of receptivity to awareness of a deeper realization of self. He refuses us the right to hide behind the skepticism that lives in man's questioning of the possibilities of knowledge, to accept the fateful consequence of a mortality limited to itself. He rejected the pessimism that reduced our hopes to resignation and our moral visions to a desperate search for salvation, an escapism that ends in moral degeneracy.

With tolerance for experiences that are different from our own, and not subject to that critical intelligence that we have learned to adore, the philosopher can again undertake to open philosophy to the love of wisdom. Philosophy would no longer be one experience among others, but would again be the end and purpose of all the activities of life. We should remind ourselves that it was Aristotle in the Metaphysics who taught us that knowledge begins in wonder: "It is through wonder," he said, "that men now begin and originally began to philosophize; wondering in the first place at obvious perplexities, and then by gradual progression raising questions about the greatest matters...."[25]

---

[24]*Ibid.*, 119.
[25]Metaphysics I, II, 9-10 (Cambridge, Harvard University Press, 1975).

We began with Bergman's critique of Jaspers's philosophical faith. Bergman's critique was a statement of his own conception of philosophy. Bergman believed that human reason which is not confronted by receptivity to divinity, is inadequate to give man a purpose, to create the future as the source of hope and love. Bergman pleaded for a philosophical openness that made it possible for us to be sensitive to experiences that are different from those that are habitual or which satisfy an accepted point of view. A courageous philosophy reveals to mankind the unfathomable nature of the future, and causes us to be open to a mankind that has not yet begun to explore its possibilities, to realize that its consciousness is slowly undertaking its journey towards its fulfillment and that communication with higher powers is an integral part of its destiny. This is a courageous and beautiful optimism. Bergman gives us those "droplets of light" which allow us to emerge from the limitation which we often find so natural and comfortable. Be courageous, Bergman advises us, we have only just begun the philosophical endeavor. Our trust and courage will open new and limitless horizons for us. With reverence, we will grasp the meaning of man's partnership with God.

3

A Friendship of Decades

Hugo Bergman traveled many paths which always found peaceful relationships with each other. He sought to follow the path of the academic life, that of the political and social thinker, but above all, he tried to penetrate those worlds of spiritual powers that made it possible for him to realize that there can be no limits to man's knowledge, feeling, and imagination. Man had that unique place in the universe which freed him from the logic of causal explanations. Man's creative powers remained beyond empirical explanations and definitions. He struggled with oppositions that defied arbitrary attempts to encapsulate him in egalitarian expressions and rights which limited him to a world of time and space and that forced him to define the limits of knowledge by the categories of phenomena. This world of empirical knowledge had its validity, but man had other journeys that would take him beyond the immediacies of his limitations, and would reveal to him divine forces that flow into the phenomenon he calls the world.

Man realizes that the world as phenomenon has no definition, that it is a possibility among others, and that its reality depends upon man's receptivity, his powers of perception and conceptualization. We listen to Socrates's question which is a revelation, and we hear things about blindness that open our souls to things above, which before seemed unknown and hidden from us. Socrates's questions intended to reveal higher realms of reality: "Do you think," he said, "that there is any appreciable difference between the blind and those who are veritably deprived of the knowledge of the veritable beings of things, those who have no vivid pattern in their souls and so cannot, as painters look to their models, fix their eyes on the absolute truth, and always with reference to that ideal and in the most exact possible contemplation of it, establish in this world also the laws of the beautiful, the just and the good, when that is needful, or guard and preserve those that are established?"[1]

Philosophers had always known that there were realities greater than the shadows or appearances we believed constituted the existence of the world. Bergman, in his early thirties, had come to know through the figure of Rudolf Steiner (1861-1925), that there were realms of reality that man had yet to reach and embrace. Man was always going forth to new "lands" of perception for which he had to prepare both his intellect and imagination. These "lands" had to be seen and for this man needed new "heights" and powers of imagery. Again it is Plato who gave us the directions in his immortal "Allegory of the Cave." There is always the need for a release from the fetters that have held man to his old "lands" and habitual perceptions. "What would be the manner of the release and healing," Socrates observed, "from these bonds and this folly, if in the course of nature something of this sort should happen to them: When one was freed from his fetters and compelled to stand up suddenly and turn his head around and walk, and to lift up his eyes to the right, and in doing all this, felt pain and, because of the dazzle and glitter of the light, was unable to discern the objects whose shadows he formerly saw, what do you suppose would be his answer if someone told him that what he had seen before was all a cheat and an illusion, but that now, being nearer to reality and turned toward more real things, he saw more truly?"[2]

Bergman sought to return philosophy to its primordial love, to that love of wisdom which brought it beyond the various divisions that vie for its possession. Philosophy never followed the sciences, it always preceded them. Now we begin with the sciences and bring philosophy to them as if they needed the help of this ancient wisdom. Philosophy seems weakened and dispensable as a handmaid. The consolation it offers itself is inadequate. It needs again the myths that brought forth its metaphysics, its search for immortality, the nature of the human soul, but above all, love of ideas and the powers that are in them. In these ancient teachings, philosophy stood above the arts and sciences, the technologies of man's inquisitiveness and was the refuge of the ultimate question of human life. Philosophy stood close to divinity. We have learned to speak of philosophy in the genitive mood as if she belonged to history or science, to art or politics. Philosophy refers only to herself; she contemplates the logic of her own thinking, she looks backwards upon herself and comprehends that thinking upon thinking that is the essence of Being. This self-reflection is the *reprise*, a relearning and deepening of

---

[1] *The Republic* (Cambridge, Harvard University Press, 1946), Book VI, 484 C-D.
[2] *Ibid.*, Book VII, 515 D-E.

A Friendship of Decades

a reality that has defied definition and fixed rules of expression. Philosophy is the openness to what was and will be. These remain fluid and rest upon realms of reality that philosophy is forever exploring and revealing. Bergman called upon us to grasp a simple truth: "the consciousness of today is only a small sector of a whole range of possible awareness...."[3] The horizons of philosophy would then swing open to possibilities that would deeply affect and challenge thinking and the imagination.

Bergman remarked that the Kant which he studied in his youth, the theorist of knowledge, the creator of the Transcendental Aesthetic, the philosopher who had revealed time and space as the elements of knowing, had yielded to the Kant of the Transcendental Dialectic, the Kant of the Antinomies, but, above all, the Kant who could not let go of the "architectonic interest of reason" and who could clearly state: "Human reason is by nature architectonic."[4] Kant added to this powerful affirmation the insight that human reason "regards all our knowledge as belonging to a possible system, and therefore allows such principles as do not at any rate make it impossible for any knowledge that we may obtain to combine into a system with other knowledge. But the propositions of the antithesis are of such a kind that they render the completion of the edifice of knowledge quite impossible."[5]

The openness of reason, its capacity to freely and constructively reveal new paths of knowing, is now set before the thinker. He walks from the cave into the sunlight, dazzled by its brightness he feels the pain and the strength of its revelatory powers. The limits that were justly imposed upon our phenomenological knowledge are removed for the reason that brings to this knowledge new ways of understanding, new dimensions of conceptualization, and the expansive powers of the imagination. The reason informs man that he is not limited to phenomena, there are other sources of knowing, and that the consciousness and conscience that man so deeply values have only just begun to be explored. The future bears new realities that men have only just begun to realize. Men must risk their limits for new realities.

Man must free himself from the propositions that what cannot be proved empirically is necessarily false and of no value. Kant, at a moment of literary and speculative exuberance, made it very clear that "if men could free themselves from all such interests, and consider the assertions of reason irrespective of their consequences, solely in view of

---

[3]*The Need for a Courageous Philosophy*, 119.
[4]*Kant's Critique of Pure Reason*, trans. N.K. Smith (New York, Humanities Press, 1950) B-502.
[5]*Ibid.*

the intrinsic force of their grounds, and were the only way of escape from their perplexities to give adhesion to one or other of the opposing parties, their state would be one of continuous vacillation.... If, however, they were summoned to action, this play of the merely speculative reason would, like a dream, at once cease, and they would choose their principles exclusively in accordance with practical interests."[6]

Everything is subject to our action and our awareness that knowledge is existential and meaningful. We are only limited to the limits of our awareness. We agree with Bergman when he said that "there is no judging the world at all, because the world is a phenomenon; it is not fixed and it dangles in nothingness. We are summoned to listen and to hear the message that speaks to us from out of the world. The being of the world is not being in itself; it is within the world and through the world that the word of God is carried out. It is in the world, in time, that the meeting of God and man takes place, the meeting of the eternal within us and the external in itself."[7]

The assumptions we make about freedom, about the relationship between truth and existence depend upon how deeply we feel about the living quality of truth, the *fact* that we are willing to act upon, and construct from it, a philosophy that shows how deeply truth and existence belong to each other, how intimate is the relationship between man and God, and how creatively we develop that partnership between God and man in the concreteness of time and space. These elements not only describe the phenomenological qualities of knowledge, but they are equally the sources of that interplay of opposites in and through which the mortal and the immortal touch and relate to each other.

Kant knew that we not only have to decide and act *as if* the truth we affirm is the truth, but that we must also speculate about the paradoxes that constitute human life. "It is fitting," he said, "that a reflective and enquiring being should devote a certain amount of time to the examination of his own reason, entirely divesting himself of all partiality and openly submitting his observations to the judgment of others. No one can be blamed for, much less prohibited from, presenting for trial the two opposing parties, leaving them, terrorized by no threats, to defend themselves as best they can, before a jury of like standing with themselves, that is, before a jury of fallible men."[8]

We are pleased by Kant's willingness to allow philosophy to belong to the public arena and to find there the forum of debate, but the interest of reason goes beyond debate to a commitment to truth from which other

---

[6]*Ibid.*, B-503.
[7]"The Need for a Courageous Philosophy," 105.
[8]*Critique of Pure Reason*, B-504.

realities emerge. The more difficult and challenging experience of life is the realization that faith precedes knowledge and that philosophy is ultimately faith not in reason, but in the presence of the light, i.e., in God. Plato reminded us that the sun is to our eyes as faith is to the source of the creativity of the spirit. In the *Laws*, he stated that "in our eyes God will be 'the measure of all things' in the highest degree – a degree much higher than in any man they talk of." Plato then reminded us that "to engage in sacrifice and communion with gods continually by prayers and offerings and devotions of every kind is a thing most noble and good and helpful towards the happy life and superlatively fitting also, for the good man, but for the wicked, and very opposite."[9] Deeply ingrained in both Plato and Aristotle is the truth that the measure of reality is divinity, and that man seeks to find the traces of this reality in all that he learns, feels and wills.

In Kant, Bergman found that "interests of humanity" to be an impetus for man's journeys to worlds of wonder that could only be restrained by his natural limitations, the boundaries of his visions. In Kant, there lived two souls, one belonged to the epistemologist, the other lived with the awareness of man's unbounded need for metaphysics. With a respect for each other and a clear recognition of the justice of the activities, Kant was able to bring them alongside each other without arbitrarily confusing them. "The hope of *a future life*," Kant remarked, "has its source in that notable characteristic of our nature, never to be capable of being satisfied by what is temporal (as insufficient for the capacities of its whole destination); the consciousness of *freedom* rests exclusively in the clear exhibition of duties, in opposition to all claims of the inclinations; the belief in a wise and great *Author of the world* is generated solely by the glorious order, beauty, and providential care everywhere displayed in nature."[10] Philosophy, unlike mathematics, is not an armed and impregnable fortress. Philosophy has its source in what is characteristic of man's unlimited power of both wonder and the exactitudes of knowledge. In some subtle way, the embrace of philosophy brings these varied elements into a meaningful whole.

Bergman noted that in the same book Kant's desire "to lay the philosophical foundations for the natural sciences and to destroy the belief in the reality of the world, was doubtless one of the greatest wonders of the spirit, but most of the philosophies of our time have not had the power to encompass this wonder in its entirety, and they have

---

[9]*Laws* (London, William Heinemann, 1952) B.IV 716 A-B.
[10]*Critique of Pure Reason*, B XXXIII.

sacrificed the metaphysical basis on the altar of a theory of knowledge."[11]

If men have not always sought a knowledge of God, and the powers that govern our world, it is because men have found it difficult to escape their temporal existence and its unbearable incarceration. Between the philosophies of Wolff and Hume, Kant suggests at the end of the *Critique,* that we follow a critical path, but he indicated that this path is as yet incomplete. We have yet "to secure for human reason complete satisfaction in regard to that with which it has all along eagerly occupied itself though hitherto in vain."[12]

What Bergman showed the philosophers was in many ways similar to Kant. If philosophy is the love of wisdom, then the powers which it embraces transcend the varied aspects of philosophical studies; it precedes the creation of the arts and sciences; it forges the Ideas which it discovers to be the "Light" of its thinking, seeing, and hearing, and it realizes that its awareness is rooted in those world-governing powers that defy the possibilities of knowledge and at the same time cause it to know the dissatisfaction which these limitations create in it.

In the *Critique of the Power of Judgment,* Kant showed how the investigation of the parts of an instrument do not reveal the cause of that same instrument. He observed that "the producing cause of the watch and its form is not contained in the nature of this material, but lies outside the watch in a being that can act according to ideas of a whole which its causality makes possible."[13] In other words, the formation of living reality cannot be explained from itself and every attempt of science to find embracing laws of causality end in failure. Reality is not governed by its own law, but is dependent upon forces that influence it from above. The world is not the creation of the laws which man brings from himself, but is constantly being formed from the relationship between the higher and the lower powers that are secretly tied to each other. If the world is a phenomenon, then it is in constant creation, and the governing forces which control its reality are constantly being realized in man's awareness that what he seeks to understand is dependent upon his capacity to be receptive to what comes to him from above and beyond himself. The world exists in the presence of God, in the presence of spiritual powers that affect its movement and determine its reality, not only in the form of causality, but from that "synchronicity" of forces which Carl Jung fruitfully developed. As soon as we liberate

---

[11]"The Need for a Courageous Philosophy," 109.
[12]*Critique of Pure Reason,* B 884.
[13]*The Critique of Judgment,* trans. J.C. Meredith (Oxford, Oxford University Press, 1969) #65.

A Friendship of Decades

ourselves from the prejudices of our technical superiority, which we now translate into spiritual predominance, we will be able not only to seek explanations which proceed from the lower to the higher, but we can again regain that movement that goes from the higher to the lower."

Opening a new dimension of reality, Bergman noted that "the self of a human being existed before it entered the body." This was the Idea of Plato and supported by Goethe. Bergman explained that this "hypothesis that the self of man exists before it takes on flesh and blood, perfectly explains the essence of the human self and its biography."[14] Bergman assented to the idea that the self of the individual existed before it entered the body. He did not indicate that he also accepted the continuity of the soul from one life to another as was explained in the "Myth of Er," but he was more inclined to be sympathetic with the thinker Rudolf Steiner, whose works he read throughout his life.

Steiner, in his *Theosophy, An Introduction to the Supersensible Knowledge of the World and the Destination of Man*, stated that "as physical man I spring from other physical men because I have the same shape as the whole human species. The qualities of the species, accordingly, could thus be acquired only within the species. As spiritual man, I have my own shape just as I have my own biography. I can have obtained the shape, therefore, from no other but myself. I did not enter the world with undefined, but with defined soul-predispositions, and since the course of my life as it comes to expression in my biography is determined by these predispositions, my work upon myself cannot have begun with my birth. That is to say, I must have existed as spiritual man before my birth."[15]

The sanctity of every man lies in the uniqueness of his spiritual origin and the biography that is written for him from this origin. Man is the only being who writes his autobiography, but this he does from the predisposition with which he entered the world. The soul has a divine origin, embodies in itself a spark of God and bears this divinity through the course of his life; it is the unextinguishable reality of life that makes each man become a particular partner with God in the continuous creation of the universe. In the soul, man finds the undefinable and inexplicable element of human existence. Material existence is deprived of its dominance over man's condition. Man discovers again and again that he is more than the instincts and inclinations that rule the lives of the animals. Man's uniqueness resides in this spiritual soul quality that has not come from him, but from a source other than himself.

---

[14]"The Need for a Courageous Philosophy," 115.
[15]*Theosophy, An Introduction to the Supersensible Knowledge of the World and the Destination of Man*, (New York, Anthroposophic Press, 1988), 52.

Bergman was fond of quoting Goethe who remarked that "'from my father I have the stature and the serious manner of life; from my mother, a joyous disposition and the love of romance.' Genius, of course he did not receive from either."[16] What is significant about these observations is their denial of man's attempt to explain his reality through material or historical explanations. Man's spiritual life depends upon that movement from higher worlds to the lower worlds, from the divine hierarchy to man. The self-enclosed world that is created through a causal logic that refuses to be open to synchronicity, to the presence of higher powers and to the *fact* that there is an intimate relationship between the governing forces of the universe and man's reality, fails to allow man to face the "Light" that gives him new possibilities of perceiving and conceiving.

For nearly sixty years, Bergman remained a reader of Rudolf Steiner. It was a radical departure from his academic writings, his translations of Kant and Hermann Cohen, his writings on Schelling and his grand history of philosophy from the Renaissance to Kant and Idealism. Behind these works lay other speculations and, in particular, a devotion to Steiner. In an introduction to Steiner's work *The Philosophy of Spiritual Activity, Fundamentals of a Modern View of the World,* Bergman set forth his evaluation of Steiner. In this introduction lies one of the basic elements of Bergman's thought. We discover after long years of study of Bergman's thought, that there are many faces to his work and beliefs. Steiner was a constant influence because there were beliefs that both men shared. They believed that man had a spiritual destiny that was present in his soul and was revealed to man in his refusal to allow any materialistic or vaguely mystical doctrine to hinder his attempts to discover the interrelationship between perception and conceptualization. Bergman affirmed repeatedly that "man's evolution toward this highest goal (the realization of his freedom), is far from completed: Man has not yet become a reality."[17] This openness to the spirit, the search for the meaning of it and the attempt to show how deeply philosophy is involved in revealing to mankind the vast forces of the human spirit and their dependence on yet other powers, became the quiet but inexhaustible and original work of Hugo Bergman.

At the beginning of his "Introduction," Bergman showed Steiner's unique place in Western thought. He stated that "in the history of recent Western philosophy, Rudolf Steiner appears as a unique personality because his whole philosophical work is not the result of a thinking

---

[16]*Ibid.,* 57.
[17]*The Philosophy of Spiritual Activity* (New York, Rudolf Steiner Publications, 1963), Introduction by Hugo Bergman, (1961), 25.

A Friendship of Decades

effort, but is based on spiritual experiences. In the world of the East, it goes without saying that a great thinker is at the same time a great initiate; in the West, however, it never before occurred that a whole philosophical system was based on immediate spiritual experience. For this reason, Steiner had to face the greatest mistrust from the world of the 'official' philosophers."[18] The latter world was Bergman's for the whole of his life, but it was not his only world. He knew the world of the East and he knew the philosophers who attempted to embrace both worlds. Bergman always liked the metaphor of "the bridge." His life was a series of bridges which he forged between the varieties of religious experiences which he believed bore witness to man's never-ending struggle to respond to the presence of God. His work was a partnership which he extended to all those who believed that there were many dimensions to the human-divine confrontation. Steiner was a spiritual companion whom he could never leave. Steiner awakened him to spiritual possibilities that he did not open to himself, but for which he was sensitive and could hear with sympathy and appreciation. The genius of Bergman lay in his extraordinary sensitivity to varieties of thought which for him were the never-ending expressions of the spirit. Bergman was not a follower of any doctrine. He walked alongside those with whom he spoke, stopped when he could no longer follow, and waited until the dialogue could begin again. His receptivity made the continuity at times possible, and at others, he would yield to his inability to experience the high in realities which he was not at the moment prepared to confront. His life was a continuous preparation.

Bergman described Steiner's attitudes with great clarity. Their relationship went beyond intellectual appreciation – although Bergman many times described it in this manner – it was founded in the reality of similar experience. Bergman took offense when Buber was critical of Steiner in a way that Bergman found to be improper, and Buber offered his apologies. Bergman described Steiner's identification of the world of the senses and the spiritual with admirable simplicity: "We are by no means," he said, "separated from the realities of the world forever, but only as long as we are perceiving by means of the senses exclusively. Actually, the world of the senses is spiritual. If by enhancing our soul life, we succeed in experiencing the ideas working in the world of senses, then we are able to experience the world in its reality. Steiner calls his philosophical system 'concrete' or 'objective idealism.'"[19]

In editing the natural scientific works of Goethe, Steiner introduced the reader to the direction his future work would take. He remarked in

---

[18]*Ibid.*, 11.
[19]*Ibid.*, 12.

his book, published in English as *Goethean Science*, that "his subject has no other task than that of arranging the object in such a way that it discloses its innermost nature. 'The true is Godlike, it does not appear directly, we must divine it from its manifestations.' The point is to bring their manifestations into such a relationship that the 'true' appears. The true, the *idea*, already lies within the fact which we confront in observation; we must only remove the covering that conceals it from us. The true scientific method consists in the removing of the covering. Goethe took this path and we must follow him upon it if we wish to penetrate completely his nature."[20] In these remarks, we anticipate lines of thinking that became known in the work of Martin Heidegger.

The opposition that we have created by speaking of subject and object, destroyed the reality of the object. We either affirmed that human consciousness cannot be enhanced, or that all knowledge depended upon powers of the knowing subject to impose its attitudes and categories upon the external world. Kant noted in a significant footnote to section 91 of the *Critique of the Power of Judgment*, that "faith is a confidence in the moral law. But this promise is not regarded as one involved in the moral law itself, but rather as the one which we impose into it...."[21]

We have learned to accept the *fact* that through the imposition of the thinking *I*, we create nature, give it new dimensions, purposes and history. Nature is helpless without man the creator, and yields easily to his will and impressions. In this respect, man conceals the presence of God, the independence of nature's formative powers, and the *fact* that man is true to his reality, a creative restorer, an active participant whose activity reflects movements and developments which are synonymous with living nature. What man sees, hears or touches, no longer shows his passivity, the consequences of effects which he doesn't control, but to which he only reacts. Man, as he learned his powers of conceptualization, his productive imagination, began to realize that there was an analogy between him and God. Delighted with these inscrutable powers, man transformed his knowing and will into autonomous powers in response for the subjugation he believed was imposed upon him by nature. His analogy with God was easily assumed to enhance his image.

Bergman explained the new reality that was discovered by Goethe: "Man," he said, "has to let things speak to him in a twofold way: one part of this reality is given him without his cooperation, if only he opens his senses; the other part, however, can be grasped by him by means of his thinking only, and if he is blessed as was Goethe, he is able to see it

---

[20]*Goethean Science* (New York, Mercury Press, 1988), 97.
[21]*Critique of Judgment*, #91, 146.

A Friendship of Decades

with his very eyes. However, together the two parts form the complete whole of the object itself."[22] Man is a receptive being who knows that there is life all about him, visible in varied forms, realizing laws of life that man did not create, but from which man learned the meaning of life in its varied and multiple manifestation. Man's longing to relate to nature as God is related to him, causes radical distortions in the relationships. Nature is a divine creation, bearing in itself the principles of its life. Man similarly bears within him the nature of his existence, but the latter remains beyond his powers of judgment, and man cannot avoid speculations about the possibilities of knowledge. This condition reflects the temporary reality of man's spatial and temporal conditions. The latter is, however, not absolute and the consciousness of it grows and develops in time. Man's conscious life has only begun to reveal the possibilities of its realities. The history of human consciousness has only just begun, and in these beginnings we witness the oppositions between subject and object, sense and spirit, percept and concept. Bergman longed for a humanity that would one day accept its partnership with God, which could embody his Law and stand before that eschatological event, called the Day of the Messiah, wit hope and courage.

If for Kant, the postulates of God, Immortality, and Freedom, were the "adventures of reason," the same was not true for either Goethe or Steiner. "How," Bergman asks, "is man able to grasp this idea which, of its own nature is non-physical, yet working in the physical world of the senses? Goethe considered himself as possessing a power of judgment by looking at an object – an *anschauende Urteilskraft*; he says that the thinking itself must be metamorphosed, must be enhanced, in order to experience the idea of metamorphosis. A spiritual activity is needed, a dynamic thinking."[23]

Bergman spoke of the enhancement of thinking, and the words sound important, but we wonder about this enhancement. Man is asked to leave the bounds that are well known to him, and whenever he does, he is aware that those about him will view his attempts with skepticism and scorn. Men find it difficult to go beyond the lands they know well. They prefer to study what is before them, rather than go beyond the given limitation they have known during their lives. What is known conforms to the traditional duality of percept and concept. We only ask if such a duality truly exists and is it dependent upon man's peculiar habits of knowing. If man's thinking only artificially belongs to how we know, then we must again think of the experience that speaks of the possibilities of knowledge, and inquire about their validity.

---

[22]*The Philosophy of Spiritual Activity*, 15.
[23]*Ibid.*, 16.

If the opposition between percept and concept is only the consequence of man's subjective thinking, then how do we grasp the essence of the senses? Bergman stated that "science is by no means a mere repetition of what is presented to us by the senses in some abbreviated form, but rather it adds to it something fundamentally new, something which can never be found in the mere perception, or in experience. This fundamentally new principle, however, is by no means something of a subjective nature which, according to Kant, man projects on the given perception, or on nature, but rather the true essence of the world of the senses itself. The physical phenomena are riddles which the thinking solves; but what this thinking brings about is the objective world itself. For the world is presented to us by two means, by sense perception *and* by spiritual knowledge. Both are parts of the objective world."[24]

Man restores unity to what he believed was duality. He reveals the spiritual content that lies within things. Rather than the isolation of subject and object, man restores the unity of thinking and perceiving. In this unity, man is not only the restorer, but also a creator. Without man, i.e., without thinking, nothing would exist. We would not comprehend how thinking and the senses belong to each other. Thinking is something that embraces us and it is only in the manner that we can think of ourselves as the possessors of thought. We possess thought only because we are already possessed by it. We separate the senses from thinking only because the separation is already overcome in thinking itself. Man is therefore a discoverer of reality, but in no way is a discovery analogous to divine creation.

Bergman claimed that Steiner succeeded in constructing a meaningful *objective* idealism. "What is new in Kant's philosophy," he said, "his idealism in contrast to dogmatism, remains in Steiner's world conception. Steiner, however, refuses to accept the *subjective* nature of this idealism and with it, the disastrous division of the world into that of human experience and that of objects in themselves. For Steiner, thinking is neither a mere subjective activity, nor a shadowy imitation of the perception, but an independent spiritual reality."[25]

If we assume that men are possessed by this spiritual thinking, then we can assume that there is "one spiritual cosmos" to which all men belong. Man can only begin his liberation which does not belong to a mechanical development or process by an act of faith. Steiner leaves us with a philosophical experience of self-liberation, but it remains inadequate as long as it is not preceded by the commitment of faith. No

---
[24]*Ibid.,* 17.
[25]*Ibid.,* 20.

A Friendship of Decades

matter how deeply Bergman found himself tied to Steiner, no matter how fundamentally he believed that "the evolution of mankind *as a whole* within the hierarchy of the Spiritual Beings is a process of *cosmic* importance,"[26] there was the act of faith that made everything possible. This was absent in Steiner.

Faith is never the subject of debate and question. We cannot approach Bergman's thought without returning to the foundation of all thought, to faith. He set forth the nature of this foundation in a short article, "Koennen wir glauben?" (Can We Believe?). His words revealed the force that drove his thought from level to level of reality, to dwell with faith wherever he found it. He remarked that "it is a sign of the times how much Hitler has inwardly overcome us, how 'he has overpowered the Queen in our own home.' In the last years Auschwitz has been used as an argument against our faith in God. Were the six million that Hitler killed sinners? Could they have saved themselves by their trust in God? Never could such questions be posed by the believer, and faith is, for this reason, not there to answer them. Faith is not an historical or sociological theory. Faith is power, certainty, trust and assurance."[27]

From there we proceed with our philosophical work, for we know that without them there is no philosophy, no love of wisdom, and no measure for what is right or wrong, true or false. Bergman remained like the old Tertullian, a believer in knowledge, but only if this latter found its foundation in faith. He never identified faith with any particular historical religion. He knew that it had varied forms and to these each man developed an openness. He prayed to have the strength to comprehend his faith. Prayer gave him the force to remain open to the presence of God's spirit.

---

[26]*Ibid.*, 26.
[27]"Mitteilungsblatt" (Jerusalem), September 18, 1963, 4.

4

Members of the Community of Israel

On June 25, 1938, Hugo Bergman wrote a letter to a well-known and admired Swiss theologian, Leonhard Ragaz (1868-1945). The letter began with these words: "There are only a few people in hebraic Palestine who know your name and your influence, but these few do not want to fail to acknowledge your 70th birthday and to say thanks for what they have received from you. What have we received from you? You have taught us to understand better and deeper our sense of peoplehood and the remaining of our personal existence."[1] Bergman would explain what he owed to Ragaz, but I would also like to ask about him, and understand why he was so significant for Bergman. He was one of the most significant and influential Swiss theologians, an opponent of Karl Barth's dialectical theology, one of the great leaders of religious socialism, a close friend of Martin Buber and a powerful personality. He published meaningful and original books among which I would like to cite: *Weltreich, Religion und Gottesreich* (1922). These two volumes were reviewed by Buber in 1923. His most widely known book was *Von Christus zu Marx – Von Marx zu Christus* (1929). The book that is central for our discussion is: *Israel Judentum Christentum* (1943). Let us not forget his journal, *Neue Wege*, in which there are treasures of theological debate and analysis. We go back to World War I to the writings of Buber on nationalism and Zion, visions of community, universality and biblical faith that linked him closely to Ragaz and his sublime belief in the presence of the Kingdom of God.

Bergman possessed a gift of receptivity. He knew how to listen. He was a Pythagorean listener; he did not listen passively. This listening was the opening of new paths – the sources of creative syntheses and expansive visions. He chose not to build systems. His life was a

---

[1]*Tagebuecher & Briefe*, Vol. I, 1901-1948, 6/25/38.

constant development; it was as if the spirit filled him again and again with ever-new revelations and made it impossible for him to believe that he had found the singular, all-embracing truth which he could proclaim with consistency and regularity. This does not say that there were no important and precious truths that captured and guided his, but these always found new forms.

Bergman visited Ragaz during a European trip in 1936. He had read widely in the Ragaz literature, but the visit in 1936 made the personal impression which is never possible through books. Bergman described the meeting on August 31: "His personal impression was at first severe; there was a deep religiosity, an inner faith and a certain aloofness; a sharp sense of fate burdened him. If the World War would come and the German entered Zurich, he saw the dire fate of Switzerland and only a miracle could save her. She would disintegrate inwardly; no leading socialist individual would save her. All this made a dire impression. Striking was his belief in Palestine, in the Jewish people, in the strength of the individual, in spite of mass existence. Who knows, perhaps the fate of Palestine depends on both of you." (Bergman was accompanied by S. Schocken.)[2]

Bergman was always deeply impressed by faith. He knew that it was one of those gifts rarely given man. It was that undefined power that allowed man to live in defiance of the weaknesses that drew him into common existence. Faith was the binding that tied every believer to his Father Abraham. Bergman's faith joined the faith of others. This was the peculiarity and uniqueness of his existence. He lived in a rare dependence upon others. He believed through their faith, as others believed through his. This was the community of belief that emerged from his philosophy and became the reality of his thought and existence. Bergman could never be separated from the prophetic faith, from vision and hope, but this feeling and devotion was never a substitute for work and social and political engagement. He belonged fully to political and social activity. He knew that only in effort and activity could the ideal be brought about. Its reality lay in the force and goodness of work. This was not spiritual, but physical work, work on the land and in community. In this work, the spiritual and physical become one, the oneness that is their originative power.

After speaking of the importance of liberal Judaism and its great representative Hermann Cohen, Bergman mentioned to Ragaz its inadequacies. "They did not see the bodily, spiritual and political reality of the Jewish person and mass, and in its anticipatory expectation of a messianic event wanted to erase the differences between Israel and the

---

[2]*Ibid.*, 8/31/36.

nations. It unwillingly became the tool of the Jewish assimilation movement which threw off the yoke of its own peculiar existence."[3]

Bergman, with all his genuine idealism, remained a thinker who was fully aware that physical existence was a sanctified way of life. His idealism never severed the physical from the spiritual reality. From the totalitarian forms of government, this work ethic had little chance to emerge. Bergman believed deeply in the value and redemptive powers of the individual, and he saw in every genuine human activity, the redemptive nature of work, a means by which man expressed his gratefulness to the Creator to whom all belonged. Hermann Cohen had not understood what it meant to build a land, the preparatory work for the coming of the Messiah. Messianism was not the creation only of the mind; it belonged equally to the hands, those beautiful instruments of creativity and love.

Bergman stated that Zionism and nationalism were the necessary instruments through which the people could find again their land and their history. "The national and Zionist movement," Bergman stated, "to which we belong and from which we emerge, realized the corporeal existence and need of our people."[4] The goal of this Zionism had been clearly stated by Buber in an essay of reply to Hermann Cohen in 1917. "My goal," he wrote, "is not one more tiny entity of power in the throng. What I want is a settlement that, independent of the machinery of nations, and removed from external politics, can focus all its energy upon the inner life and thereby, the realization of Judaism.... We want Palestine not 'for the Jews,' we want it for humanity. We want it for the realization of Judaism. The work of the new humanity we intend cannot do without the specific power of Judaism, the power that once gave mankind its strongest impulse for true life."[5] Idealism, Utopianism, Nationalism, are terms we could apply to these realities, showing how unaware we are of the realism of power politics, and how naive are the believers in dreams of universalism and the faith in mankind. Bergman, with his great sense of receptivity, would hear with sympathy the words of realism, understand them and agree to them, but he heard other voices, those of his friend Buber, those of the prophets and those who came to the land with faith and hope. He heard and knew there were truths in all that was said, that in some way they could live together if

---

[3]*Ibid.*, 6/25/38.
[4]*Ibid.*
[5]"Zion, the State, and Humanity," published in *Der Jude* (1916-1917), now in *The Jew: Essays from Martin Buber's Journal Der Jude, 1916-1928* (Philadelphia, Jewish Publication Society, 1980), 93.

they were not bound or assimilated to each other. Human existence is the living together of opposites. Bergman knew this well.

Bergman revealed to Ragaz how the political necessities of the day easily pushed back the spiritual elements, and, at times, suffocated them. He was saddened to see how easily the immediacies of life easily take precedence over man's spiritual concerns. He stated to Ragaz: "The corporeal, social and national interests force their way into the foreground with a vigor and power that Israel had not known. Political persecutions cause a weakening of the meaning for what is essential."[6]

Bergman, like Ragaz, was a man who lived from the realities of existence. Neither formulated thoughts from the pulpit or the podium. They were men who fought the battles of daily existence in journals, letters and speeches. These were not sedentary souls. They were fighters for the spirit. They were devoted to the creation. They saw themselves as co-creators, men in the service of divinity. Each knew that his work could bring closer the Kingdom of God.

In his final remarks to Ragaz, Bergman spoke of Israel's needs. He said that what "Israel needs today is the weighed distinction of means and goal. The means whose most distinguishing characteristic is our own existence has the tendency to become independent and to allow the goal to be forgotten: the religious sense of our existence. It is in this regard Herr Ragaz, that we are so thankful to you. You have always recalled us to the religious meaning of Israel."[7]

Bergman was not hesitant to thank a Christian theologian for his insistence upon the religious meaning of Israel. Those who are too close to their reality, at times forget the goal for the sake of the means. But what is of greater importance, is the universal community of believers who are dependent upon each other. The openness to the Christian Ragaz, is as valuable and significant as that to the Indian Sri Aurobindo, to Rav Kook, to the theosophist Frithjof Schuon, to the Muslim René Guénon, to the voice of his friends Martin Buber, Gershom Scholem, Ernst Simon, Felix and Robert Weltsch. The mystery of Bergman's fabulous capacity to listen goes beyond the imagination. He never became a storehouse of knowledge, nor an endless series of quotations; he created a process of learning that defied the understanding and forced it again and again to surpass itself. He gave meaning to the *complexio oppositorum* showing how opposites lived together in a mutually beneficial manner. This mystery goes beyond our imagination but, at the same time, it stimulates and excites it. We witness the powers listening,

---

[6] *Tagebuecher*, 6/25/38.
[7] *Ibid.*

and we wonder if they do not hear in themselves wonders which the speaking philosophers do not possess.

At the end of the letter, Bergman mentioned the most intimate and incisive influence of Ragaz, his appeal to the soul, that source of religious feeling and moral demand. He said to Ragaz that he "had always aroused and guarded in the soul the belief in the living God, in the coming salvation, and in realization of the Kingdom of God. You have joined through a magnificent synthesis belief in the corporeal, earthly salvation, in socialism with religious faith, and thus, given to socialism and consequently to socialistic Zionism, the deepest foundation."[8] With these words, Bergman showed how open he was to Ragaz's teaching. He knew that the deep faith of the Christian was not far from, but in fact very close to, the faith of the believing Jew and to every believer from whom man's relationship to God went beyond ritual and custom. There is good reason to recognize in Bergman's diaries and letters his most significant work. He knew that education and all the tools of learning and scholarship were empty if they didn't reveal the soul of the thinker, didn't create an openness to the spirit in all its possible manifestations. There is no word that is more difficult to use than that pronoun *I*. It is so much easier to create sophisticated external works, and so difficult to cultivate the feelings and the imagination in such a way that they become the expressions of man's deepest longings and hopes. The inner cultivation, the cultivation of the soul, belongs to man's humanity and to its revelation even more profoundly than his external and apparent achievements.

The reality of the living God which belonged to the very nature of the prophetic experience, grew even more powerful in Bergman's thinking. He spoke of a conversation which he had with his friend Felix Weltsch, an old companion from his Prague days, a friend of Franz Kafka and a distinguished philosopher. They both spoke of the need for a guide in life. The need comes forth at different times with greater and lesser intensity. Weltsch remarked: "We have the feeling in these times (1941) that we are the blind who tap around at night. Everything that a man says or thinks hardly reaches beyond the groping hand of anyone who seeks his way in the dark. I told Felix that, in the last years, I received the most help from Ragaz, the Swiss Protestant professor. I do not know if I have ever showed you his monthly *Neue Wege*. It is very Christian but so unusually strong in its God-consciousness and its God creativity, that even from the published pages a power arises, like from a dynamo."[9]

---

[8] *Ibid.*
[9] *Ibid.*, 1/27/41.

Bergman believed in the Kingdom of God whose presence he never doubted. He was profoundly aware that man travels alone, and paradoxically with companions, that ultimately the journeys were failures in their apparent achievement, but the struggles they cause and excite, are man's victories. What fails on one level is victorious on another. Man's going forth to God is the work of many men, of many faiths, and many dreams and courageous hopes. We each need someone for a guide. Man learns to rely upon man, and in turn, to be relied upon. This mutuality is the communication of the unseen community.

Ragaz's strength became Bergman's force. He learned and he taught, and in this cycle lay an astonishing capacity to embrace and be embraced, to love and to be loved. Confessional differences faded, but never disappeared; what emerged was mutuality, a rare spiritual condition which allowed the spirit to speak only because the spirit was open and receptive. The spoken word revealed reality, the sounds and inspirations that could only be gathered by a finely attuned inner receptivity. Bergman heard Ragaz and from the voice of his pages, from his love of Israel, the faith in the presence of God's Kingdom, the strength of his moral and political actions, there arose that powerful anticipation of God's presence and judgment. Faced with Nazism and anti-Semitism, Ragaz fought with the tenacity of a prophet the idolatry he found in the men near him. He rejected with thundering violence the quietism of Karl B. Barth and the ineptitude of his politics.

Ragaz, who saw Israel as God's first and eternal love, could not endure, much less tolerate, those who didn't become warriors in her behalf. Here lay Barth's failure. The struggle is always fought against the unending forms of idolatry, the awakening of the nature gods, and the self-worship which man so desperately desires and refuses to surrender. Struggle is always against reality, as we find it, against the deification of its comprehension; struggle lies in the departure from the convenient household and homeland to the new Kingdom and its demands. The struggle is to make it possible for this Kingdom to become reality in a world that resists and defies its approach.

In his book, *Weltreich, Religion und Gottesreich*, Ragaz spoke of the essence of Judaism. From 1922 to 1943, his ideas only increased in intensity and he expressed them with clearer and more forceful conviction. We have only hinted at these ideas, but if we are to comprehend Bergman's devotion to them, we must indicate their distinctness and inner strength. Bergman, as we said, was the listening thinker, and what he heard was not merely stored away to be repeated at a later date. Every idea was not clearly heard. Only those which belonged to his perception of reality influenced and conditioned his thinking. He heard with the powers of synthesis. He heard creatively;

the spirit of receptivity joined with his spontaneity to create a living thought process. What did he hear from Ragaz as he read his text? "Messianism," Ragaz stated, "which belongs to the Kingdom of God is lost to Christendom. Judaism, however, has preserved it. It must be decisively shown what the Christians have fully lost. Judaism is messianism and nothing else.... The soul of Judaism is the expectation of the Messiah, a kingdom of justice upon the earth that is brought about by God. If Judaism often hardly knows itself, if this soul seems hardly to stir in the body of Judaism, we ought not to forget that there is no stirring in the Christian truth, and in the church."[10]

Nothing saddened Bergman more than the loss of the Messianic vision in Judaism and he sought it again and again in a believing humanism which would be embraced by a community of believers from every place in the universe. Bergman lived with an ecumenism that sought to comprehend the Messianic ideal of humanity, an ideal that placed a demand before all human life and proclaimed its sanctity and inviolability.

Ragaz recognized the reality of a Jewish humanism. "Everywhere," he stated, "that we find the concept of humanity opposed to nationalism and other prejudices, the concept of humaneness opposed to brutality and subjugation, the Jews are in front. They are the most important advocates of internationalism and pacificism, of rule of law among the nations."[11] Ragaz mentioned Martin Buber, Gustav Landauer, Kurt Eisner, Hermann Cohen and Max Adler. Socialism, in the thought of these men, became hope in the oneness of humanity and a profound commitment to the realization of law and justice. With Cohen, it brought forth the reality of compassion which lay at the source of Cohen's last works. There was an awareness of the injustice of poverty, suppression and degradation. These were not empty ideas which made momentary impressions easily forgotten from one printed page to another. The struggle was always centered in national realizations, in the community and on the land. The longing for the land was always accompanied by the sanctity of work, the good of the creation and the dignity of both spiritual and physical achievement. Ragaz had a sense for the "vulcanic idealism" that lived in Judaism – often buried in it. He saw it as a yearning for the "unconditioned"; he realized how deeply it lay in the waiting for the Messiah, and how often it burst forth against the established authorities, and gave Judaism the revolutionary character it always possessed. The presence of the Messiah was the constant ground-swell against the stringent acceptance of given conditions.

---

[10] *Weltreich, Religion and Gottesreich*, 2 volumes, (Erlenbach, 1922), Vol. II, 368-369.
[11] *Ibid.*, 369.

Ragaz remained convinced that "the real, living God must break the spell of the world in order to liberate the soul and man for the divine reality.... The Kingdom of God which flows from the true God makes man free."[12] This religious idealism which found its source in man's confrontation with God, was no creation of a philosophical system which would deify the power of the concept. Here, the confrontation was historical, concrete and decisive. God's reality came forth in His confrontation, in the words of the prophets and in the events of history, in dreams, in hopes and in the sufferings of love. Above all, Bergman believed that it was the confrontation of death that determined fundamentally the depths of one's religious commitment. He spoke of death from his meditations upon Ragaz, Sri Aurobindo and Rav Kook. "Death," Bergman stated, "is not to be understood as the end, but as a point of passage, as a new beginning. Death is not an end, but a change in our conditions of consciousness; the certainty that the dead lived. Death is the great deception; the relationship of death is with Adam's sin. This sin brings about a darkening of human consciousness."[13] This overcoming of death is man's supreme longing for God, but more deeply, it is the belief in continuity, in the reality of the future. The presence of the Messiah is the source of our hope and trust; allows us to see more in life than the fate of our existence. The Messiah is presence of the promise that God's original covenant with man and creation will yield a new covenant from which evil or sin will be excluded. In the Messianic dimension of mankind, we find the purpose of our lives.

At the end of his remarks on Christianity and Judaism, Ragaz revealed the hope that lay in every religious soul for the unity of mankind. "Christ," he said, "is reconciler of East and West, of nature and spirit, law and love; he is the redemption and resurrection of all life. If in our days their oppositions grow into a new life, if Protestantism, Catholicism, Judaism and Secularism, East and West meet each other on the battlefield, and yet in the background a higher unity emerges, that is the sign that we welcome. A new life will arise. The conflicting forces will become more aware of their peculiarity and that is the presupposition of a true union."[14]

This universality became Bergman's life work. He knew it depended more upon listening to the voices of men, both present and past, than the constructions of grandiose systems of enclosed and enclosing categories. From everywhere in the universe there were men who heard the spirit and communicated the meaning of their faith; who felt tied to their

---

[12]*Ibid.*, 374.
[13]*Tagebuecher & Briefe*, 5/18/51.
[14]*Weltreich*, 375.

companions in conversation, and the written word. Bergman always reminded those about him that God loves Israel as the sign of humanity. He observed that it would be a misunderstanding to explain the anticipation of a Messianic humanity as a glorification of Israel. "The election of Israel is not an exception; on the contrary, it is the symbolic confirmation of God's love for the human race."[15] Bergman held closely the truth of prophetic Judaism. He realized that its powers were weakened by a society more concerned with immediate survival and power politics, with infinite legal studies and the clerical search for power and domination. If Ragaz was a lonely soul in Zurich, Bergman was equally an isolated being in Jerusalem.

Ragaz saw a radical opposition between the Kingdom of God and religion. He stated this clearly and precisely in 1917: "Religion is the worst of the evils. But above religion is God, the true God. He is not to be confused with it. And where one comes into relationship with him, where one comes in his light, there is his Kingdom. Where the Kingdom is, there is no serfdom, but liberation. There the demons flee.... The Kingdom of God has existed alongside and above religion throughout history. At one time, it battled with it; at another time it breathed into it something of its nature. In Israel it shone clear and victorious; in Jesus, it became the new dawn of history, Jesus Christ destroyed religion and brought the Kingdom of God to light. Jesus Christ is the end of religion. This is the greatest fact of history."[16]

Bergman believed that man had the power to sanctify creation; that it was his responsibility to do so. This responsibility proceeded from God. "Now the conscious cooperation of man," Bergman stated, "in this divine work on earth, cooperation in the realization of God's aims in the course of civilization – this is the meaning of the benediction recited to God."[17] This sanctification of creation which man recognizes in benediction became for Bergman the clarification and justification of man's work. This was not determined, defined and rigorously imposed by articles of faith; it came forth from man's realization that there is a divine human partnership, a cooperation which is embodied in the covenant and is the supreme law of the Kingdom of God. It is the law which stands before and above us, kindling in us that divine path which each must take to find his dialogue with the divine.

---

[15]"Israel and Ecumenism" (1966), 83.
[16]"Not Religion but the Kingdom of God" (1917), in *Weltreich* in *Signs of the Kingdom*, edited and translated by Paul Bock (Grand Rapids, William B. Eerdmanns Publishing Co., 1984), 38.
[17]"On Blessings," in *Ariel*, No. 30 (Jerusalem, 1973), 8.

Ragaz had the capacity to set forth his faith with clarity and conviction. Man searches constantly to find the meaning of his relationship with God. He feels deeply changes in intensity and intimacy, and he knows that whatever he says and does is a moment in a never-ending struggle for righteousness and love. For thinkers like Bergman and Buber, Zionism was a renewed attempt to understand the prophet's mission and to find the means to give it life in the creation of a new community in Palestine and Israel. But the hope transcended the location, and what was achieved would be shared with all people. Buber had spoken of a "Hebrew Humanism" that embodied the faith in the *fact* that "Israel was chosen to become a true people and that means God's people."[18] His demand could be ignored and discarded, but it could not be denied. Buber reminded us that "classical biblical man absorbs the demand for righteousness so wholly with his flesh and blood, that, from Abraham to Job he dares to remind God of it. And God, who knows that human mind and spirit cannot grasp the ways of his justice, takes delight in the man who calls him to account, because that man has absorbed the demand for righteousness with his very flesh and blood. He calls Job his servant and Abraham his beloved. He tempted both; both called him to account and both resisted temptation. That is Hebrew humanity."[19]

In this endeavor to realize the meaning of Israel as the chosen of God, both the Jew and Christian are partners. Bergman stated that "He cannot relinquish the service of either one of them." Israel belongs to both Judaism and Christianity and each seeks the realization of Israel in that constant struggle with God which creates the humanity of man. Ragaz had his own way of stating the problem and, if the vocabulary would not be Bergman's, the spirit and devotion were the same. "The real God," Ragaz said, "transcends purely human images. He comes to man and unites himself with him, but he comes from above and changes him in that act. To be sure, he thereby makes man into a true human. He is the God of justice and love, from whom comes the Kingdom. It is there he rules, and there only. It is there he appears in man, always synonymous with simple human morality, with goodness, humility, freedom, purity of heart, trust and above all, self-denial. The converse is true as well; where these virtues are, there is God, even if his name is not mentioned, and where they are not, there he is not, even if all the walls echo his name. But it is an old feeling of true men of God that God despises nothing more than the empty use of his name, hates nothing more than religion. Why does God need religion? He does not demand

---

[18]"Hebrew Humanism" (1933) in *Israel and the World, Essays in a Time of Crisis* (New York, Schocken Books, 1963), 251.
[19]*Ibid.*

religion, but rather faith and love. Religion is demanded by the gods. God demands that his will be done on earth for the god of man."[20]

Man has yearned for many earthly utopias and they have become the source of his suppression and murder. For a kingdom of god, he sought various forms of totalitarianism, but above all, self-deification and national idolatry. But the true philosophers and theologians have more than traditions; they have the living presence of divinity. Their message has been constant. God's presence is devoid of mechanical time; it is eternity. Man looks about for the many paths of endeavor. He finds that in science, literature and the arts, he is open to a vast panorama of possibilities, but each one is accompanied with the questions of purpose and meaning. Man can accept sadly the fate of his existence, seek to realize its realities, find the meaning of his identification with what *is* and discover in comprehension the means to make it viable and livable. Man can also seek the fullness of the ethical responsibility and accept the judgment that is pronounced on human life.

Bergman spoke of a need for a courageous philosophy. This implied the capacity to stand under the divine judgment. But it is not only man that stands under and before the judgment, but history and religion. If we accept the affirmation of Ragaz that Israel is both source and foundation of Judaism and Christianity, we accept with faith that both stand under God's judgment, both have failed and are inadequate to realize the truth of Israel, the beloved and chosen of God. Judaism seeks to define the meaning of Israel. It assumes that it is Israel, the continuation of its history. Christianity makes a similar assumption and sees itself as the personification of Israel, the fulfillment and promise of the prophetic hope. Each alone is not adequate. We are faced with two distinct but complementary consequences of Israel's truth. These two paths of truth are the embodiments of Israel, ways that each must travel in their search for his divinity.

Ragaz always spoke of this reality. He rejected the simplistic and false idea of God's condemnation of Israel. In the preface to his final expression on this subject, he said: "If they want to convert them, it is not Judaism to Christianity, but, if I would presume, it should be Judaism to itself and Christianity to itself, both to each other. I am of the view that the conversion of Christianity is much closer than that of Judaism."[21]

Bergman was convinced that neither Judaism nor Christianity could or should claim totality. The rays of truth belonged to each individually,

---

[20]"Not Religion but the Kingdom of God," 33.
[21]*Israel Judentum Christentum* (Zurich, 1943), 4. *Israel, Judaism and Christianity* (London, 1947).

and each ray was a path to God. Mankind has learned the disasters that follow those who seek totality. We have learned through a long history that men who need to find exclusivity, find their destruction. Israel is a universal message; the religions that emerge from her are particular ones, with which we live as historically and traditionally conditioned people. We feel ourselves "on the way" toward a universality greater and more encompassing than the faith that prepared us for it, which we need to practice daily, and which conditions our compassion for our fellow man, and our sense of justice in nation and society. Bergman looked to the future; he was always "on the way" in his thought, but careful and caring for people, and the conditions near and about him. He pointed mankind toward that believing community in which every faith has a share if only a particular one. He often spoke of the courageous philosophy.

Bergman admitted that no Jewish thinker before him rose to the level of a Messianic humanity as did the prophets. He remarked that Franz Rosenzweig, in *The Star of Redemption* (1921), "did not even rise to the heights of Nicolaus Cusanus's (1401-1464), *Una est religio in rituum varietate*. For in spite of his profound understanding of Christianity, he had comparatively little understanding of the religions of Asia."[22] For Bergman, the words that stood before us as the eternal reality, the higher law embodied in the kingdom, were enunciated by the prophet Micah: "For all the people will walk everyone in the name of his God and we will walk in the name of the Lord our God for ever and ever" (Mic. 4:5). Closer to Bergman was Hermann Cohen's courageous belief that what God loved in Israel was mankind. Cohen stated that "it is therefore a grave mistake to evaluate the election of Israel apart from its connection with the messianic election of the human race as a whole. And this mistake entails the further one of misunderstanding the messianic election of the human race as a means for Israel's glorification. At this point, we can only point out, but nevertheless already now assert, that the election of Israel is in no way an exception but is rather the symbolic confirmation of God's love for the human race."[23] This universality flowed from Israel to both Judaism and Christianity. They both live from its glory and truth. Bergman projected the task for the future not with a system for men to study or articles of faith, but with ways for men to travel. The constant overcoming of credal stratifications and the clericalism that adheres to them was the consequence of a listening philosophy. The tasks remain those spoken of by the prophets, by Jesus and Paul.

---

[22] "Israel and Ecumenism," 83.
[23] *Religion of Reason* (New York, Frederick Ungar Publishing Co., 1972), 149.

Ragaz understood these problems well. He believed that *"Judaism and Christianity are the two branches of the tree that is called Israel. This is the decisive fact for the relationship between Judaism and Israel. From the point of view of Christianity, this had once been known; it was then forgotten. From the point of view of Judaism, it was always known, but not recognized. This fact must be seen if we want to understand the essential problem of both religions and their relationship to each other."*[24]

The task of the religions is the realization of the unseen community of faith, the suffering servant of Israel, which emerged from Israel as the beloved of God. We stand before the ancient and eternal *fides ecclesiastica*, its presence and immutable powers give light to our history and condition the nature of our lives. What is essential is the presence of this community of faith which man has not created, but in which he is transformed and given new life.

Bergman affirmed this community as a Jew, but it is confirmed by every man who hears the word of the Psalmist: "Let all that breathes praise the Lord" (Ps. 150:6). Man has a vital role in realization of the Kingdom. What other truth does the philosopher and believer tell his fellow man? He must give him no creed, no philosophical theory and no system. He knows that they will suffocate and blind him. He does not give him the powers of faith, he can only show him paths and asks him to take the responsibility which each man must assume for his travels.

Israel is God's eternal presence; it transcends every religious attempt to either define or limit it; it is more than symbol or metaphor, it is the living presence. Man approaches its meaning but falls short. Israel's reality returns man to his humanity with its inadequacy and ambiguity. Man is not leveled or narrowed in his possibilities; in fact, he is challenged to be more; he is challenged to be more human, more courageous in his confrontation with the divine.

Ragaz noted that "Israel wills in its deepest reality, not to be a religion but a world ruled by God's will and law, to be renewed and redeemed by this will and law. The Kingdom of God is the kingdom of justice, the kingdom of the fulfillment of that holy law that God puts into his creation and continuously presses upon it."[25] Ragaz removed Israel from both Judaism and Christianity, from both church and synagogue, but he has recognized their essence to be in the continuity of Israel; in their struggle to retain her message, her universality. Both Christianity and Judaism have fallen from their purpose, but each struggles again and again to retain and grasp the ancient truth that emerged from God

---

[24]*Israel Judentum Christentum*, 7.
[25]*Ibid.*, 11.

and his creation, a truth whose beginnings lie in its end, whose realization only time is able to reveal. Israel binds Judaism to Christianity and Christianity to Judaism. The separation is an idolatrous Christianity or a decadent Judaism. Each attempts to proclaim the Messiah and the faith in a Messianic humanity; they are branches alive only through the branch to which they adhere. The claims for chosenness are hidden in God's will.

"For man," Bergman said, "the election becomes an objective, an assignment that one is assigned to do. It is only God who knows the identity of those belonging to the 'mystical body' of the elect. In the place that was previously reserved for the priestly task of the Jewish people on behalf of humanity, there is now the task of God's unforeseen community, the ever expanding service of the kingdom of heaven for humanity."[26]

If Judaism and Christianity move in separate paths originating from a mutual history and emerging from the primordial truth of God's covenant, then we accept the experiences which will ever keep them apart. But why should they not travel different ways, and reveal the truths that be in Israel and have only begun to be revealed? Each path is a unique truth. If God leaves us his spirit which guides and inspires our movements and interpretations, then it is only we who are inadequate to its powers. We comprehend only from a perspective and a tradition. We don't leap from one history to another; we live with the family in which we have been born and educated and from whom we have derived our values.

Ragaz recognized the fact that "Judaism with benevolence and free conviction values Jesus as a great man, a teacher of wisdom and perhaps even as a prophet. It can recognize in the human realm his teaching and activity, but it denies the *superhuman dimension*, i.e., the miraculous birth and stresses most strongly in opposition to the Christian conception of God which culminates in the teaching of the Trinity, the oneness of God as his unique holiness."[27] Knowing the differences becomes the source of a deeper comprehension. Each must find its meaning in Israel, and each must discover in the other the source of its strength and uniqueness. Realizing that both proceed from the same body, each becomes a source of its truth and reality. Each suffers the burden of its limitation, but the suffering is the servanthood that bears witness to its history and its struggle for justification.

Ragaz refused to identify history with God. It led to the quietism that allowed men to find solace in understanding devoid of action in the

---

[26]"Israel and Ecumenism," 84.
[27]*Israel Judentum Christentum*, 24.

Members of the Community of Israel

belief that the world about them was evil. It was possible to speak of man's radical evil and to find the state as the source of a natural domination, and the relations between states controlled by the friend-foe confrontation. These doctrines have little to do with man and society. There the struggle takes place in finite freedom, in reasonableness and compromise. God's relationship to history is confrontational. In history man discovers intelligence and will, weaknesses and strengths which reveal his humanity. However we attempt to comprehend God's will in history, we are never allowed to sacrifice our reason and action for its purpose. We remain free beings. Ragaz remarked that "Israel's God is in the world as creator and judge. In *this* sense we can speak of God's becoming the world. God loves the world, God seeks the world, God wants to become one with the world. Nevertheless, He wants to remain God. That is the paradox and the secret. Just because God is other than the world, He goes into the world, and just because he goes into the world, he is God, the *living* God.... He goes as *person* to man, or more properly stated, as the man whom he sends, who accomplished his spirit. He goes as Moses to Israel, encompasses him with divine radiance. He goes as the prophets to them. He finally goes as *the* man in whom the fullness of his power and truth is embodied. He goes as the Messiah."[28] God in history is judgment and the universality of love.

The world is never consumed in doctrines that divide realms of reality from each other. Despair and radical doubt are as destructive as radical evil and resignation. The world is always meaningful and purposeful. Man's struggle for value and purpose is never vanity and fortuitousness. The philosopher remains faithful to reason and hope. The courage to preserve the dimension of the individual, the freedom of his action and judgment, was the work of Hugo Bergman. He reminded us that "the one who prays knows – with the knowledge of experience – that beyond the visible dimensions of the world, there is a hidden dimension of our existence in which something of the significance of man's being is revealed to him, revealed to a greater or lesser degree, in keeping with the strength of the communion. It is a matter of experience, and experience, as is well known, is not debatable."[29]

If there was one power that Bergman found indispensable for every life activity, it was *Devekuth*, the communion with God. With this clinging to God, man defies the anarchism that inhabits thinking, not tied to the faith in the divine. "Redemption awaits us just behind the curtain." This was Bergman's faith. He sought it in others and

---

[28]*Ibid.*, 28.
[29]"The Hope of Israel" in *The Quality of Faith* (Jerusalem, The World Zionist Organization, 1970), 61-62.

communicated with those who shared his experience and revealed to him the peculiarities of their own. His sensitivity to others was the wonder of his soul. He recognized and depended upon the truth and faith in Ragaz's work as he did with others with whom he shared these qualities. Religious and cultural differences meant little to him. He listened to Ragaz when he said, time and time again, "that Christianity and Judaism both belong to Israel. Israel lives in both (though only partly), but it is not embodied in either one, let alone in both. It flows through, over and under both. And it judges both. Israel's presence unites both and makes them allies."[30]

Bergman was the great listening thinker. He heard the many voices of the spirit. He spoke no doctrine. He taught us to be free of credal incarceration, to learn that art of hearing and realize that the word bends and must be given in such a way that those who read it are liberated and not captured by it. Man learns to be open to the presence of the light of redemption; he learns to receive the Kingdom of Heaven, which is always alive and growing in the world. Bergman, in his quiet and gentle way, faced the doubts and despair of his age with an amazing faith which he found not only in himself, but in others. This was the power of his life; he knew how to learn from others, to allow their hope and faith to fortify his. He lived community, not only in words, but in experience. He grasped the powers of dependence; the need which every man has to encounter others, to discover in relationship that wholeness which is absent in the loneliness of being, to realize that wholeness and loneliness form the vital dialectical moments that condition and determine human-divine life.

---

[30]*Israel Judaism Christianity* in *Signs of the Kingdom*, 107.

5

Cosmic Faith

Hugo Bergman was always accompanied by others in his journeys through life. Some were constant companions, and others came with him for parts of his travels. Abraham Isaac Kook (1865-1935) was a lifelong companion. He was the first Chief Rabbi of the land of Israel. Bergman wrote extensively about him. There is no doubt that his influence was significant and that Bergman's thinking absorbed deeply the visions and hopes of Rav Kook. There was another figure about whom Bergman wrote little, but whose manner of thinking impressed Bergman; this was Father Pierre Teilhard de Chardin (1881-1955). These three men, a chief Rabbi, a philosopher, and a Jesuit paleontologist, shared visions and hopes that not only changed our perspectives on man, the world, and God, but showed us new possibilities of conceiving their relationships. They brought new dimensions to faith and love; the changed perspectives challenged ways of thinking that brought with it serious opposition and, at times, violent reaction. Bergman's outwardly tranquil disposition hid the courageous positions he assumed in philosophy, politics and faith. He was always "breaking out" of dimensions of thinking that hindered his struggle for universalism, which for him was not an external vagary, but an experiential reality. Bergman's writings about these ideas are purposely scattered in articles, reviews, and commentaries. There was no book to embody a systematic expression; the flow of ideas was embodied in diaries and letters. The personal quality of thinking distinctly revealed a philosophy that developed from constant responses and meditations. Here we are privileged to witness the birth of thought and its continuous development. The responses and meditations are not chaotic but have their own peculiar order and continuity. They show that thinking is truly *reprise;* it takes up again and again what it has previously thought and reflects upon it. Every moment is an opening of a different path to the future; every moment is also the old bearing in it the truth of the past.

The belief in cosmic evolution united these thinkers. The idea dominated their attempt to incarnate it in either Judaism, philosophy or Christianity. We observe with fascination how each thinker, captivated by the Idea, attempted to make it the source of his faith. The philosopher is not the rational observer, but he is aware that the Idea needs incarnation. He grasps with appreciation how the Rabbi makes it the essence of Judaism, and how the priest finds in it the heart of Christianity, a cosmic eucharistic reality. It is, indeed, all these things, but it is more. Bergman made this clear. In his *Diary* entrance for April 5, 1948 he stated, "I have worked on Rav Kook for as long as I could. His thoughts are very bold, but always, in the worst way, narrowed and burdened with Jewish exclusivity. I have the greatest success from the study of Sri Aurobindo."[1] The same criticism could be made of Teilhard de Chardin. Both men were believers, and the Idea could not be elaborated apart from either their Judaism or their Christianity. These were the vessels into which it was poured. Bergman understood that if the historical faiths absorbed the total quantity of the Idea, a qualitative change would occur that would destroy the Idea. Neither Judaism nor Christianity are identical with cosmic evolution, but there are elements in each faith that make such interpretations possible. The idea of cosmic evolution belongs paradoxically to religion and philosophy, but it belongs to neither one nor the other exclusively.

Rav Kook's work was a continuous reflection and meditation on man's relationship to God and God's relationship to man. Within these broad dimensions lived his distinct and profound love of Israel, the Land and the Message of its history. There is a poetry in Kook's prose which reveals how deeply he was attached to the power of the Word and the Book. These were not simple tools but sources of spiritual inspiration. "The great dreams," he said, "are the foundations of the world. They are manifested on different levels. The prophets dream, as God is quoted in the saying, 'I speak with him (a prophet) in a dream' (Num. 12:8). The poets dream while awake, the mighty dream of perfecting the world. All of us dream of the time 'when God will return the captivity of Zion' (Ps. 126:1). The crudeness of conventional life, which is wholly immersed in its materialistic aspect, removes from the world the light of the dream, the splendor of its horizons, its ascent above ugly reality."[2] The great dreams emerged from that passionate struggle to find behind the

---

[1]*Tagebuecher & Briefe*, 4/5/48.
[2]*Lights of Holiness* (Vol. 1, 228) in *Abraham Isaac Kook* Trans. and Introduction Ben Zion Bokser (New York, Paulist Press, 1978).

multiplicity of man's phenomenological world a higher and deeper divine order that is hidden from us only because we have turned away from our devotion and love of God. What happens to us depends upon what we have prepared ourselves to receive. Life is a constant turning from the shadows to the light, envisioning the outflow of the higher Light towards the lower, to a world from which God has not withdrawn, but whose presence forces us to see that all is illusion that doesn't find its meaning in Him.

Bergman made a perceptive discovery through his years of study and thinking. He knew that there was a profound dialectic between the persistence of study and the qualitative changes it brings about in life. The constancy of thought doesn't only bring about a vast quantity of facts or remembrances of textual citations, but there is a radical change that occurs with the developing intimacy and love between thinkers. Bergman's relationship with Kook had much of this intimacy of silent dialogue and respect. More and more, Bergman was able to bring forth consequences from Kook's thinking about cosmic development. The latter led Bergman to a belief in ecumenism, a hope and dream that accompanied his life. He owed much to the influence of Kook. In 1972 he remarked that he had received a letter from Auroville asking him to write about Kook and Aurobindo. As he approached his ninetieth year, he noted in his *Diary*, "I must change my life, must view each day as a new beginning. I must value each day before God and judge myself before Him. Not to sleep but to learn, learn, learn, perhaps also to be a teacher for others. Put aside all vanity. Waste no time. Again to pray and learn, God will help. Learn again Rav Kook, back to Judaism as the root. Every day a principle! To be honest with myself. God will give me strength. Escha's (his wife) love helps."[3] These are the longings of a man who senses the incompleteness of all human endeavors, who knows that learning is a preparation to new insights and that each day brings with it a newness that is unpredictable and unknowable. Bergman viewed the future with hope and prayed for the courage to face what it brings. He recalled in the same *Diary* entry the words on J.G. Fichte's gravestone, "The teachers shall shine like the light of the Heaven" (Daniel 12:3). These words of Daniel marked the life of Fichte as he believed they would speak of his. Bergman would have included the words that followed, "And those who have guided the people in the true path shall be like the stars for ever and ever."

His devotion to Rav Kook emerged through the years from the boldness and daring quality of Kook's visions. If Bergman was at times unhappy with the emphasis on Jewish exclusivity and the necessary

---

[3] *Tagebuecher*, 8/15/72.

compromises, he was able to comprehend them and go beyond them. The Idea of a cosmic humanity attracted him deeply, and if the vocabulary was, at one time, Jewish or Christian, this finally meant little to him. Behind the vocabulary lived a deeper reality, a new vision of mankind's relationship to God, the Idea of the Creation drawn to its divine reality realizing within itself the essence which had been implanted in it. Man is the distinguished figure in this cosmic evolution. He bears the undefinable and unfathomable powers that transform and transfigure the universe. In him the opposites of good and evil, beauty and ugliness, struggle for reconciliation. Man, the people, or mankind harbor the powers of redemption, and it is in them that the forces of conversion and renewal have the spiritual sources for their realization.

Rav Kook remarked that "if humanity is to find its happiness and perfection in all its aspects, it is essential that these sources of light shed their radiance in full togetherness in some appropriate organic form. Thus will be resolved all spiritual problems, of individuals and of nations, in a socio-spiritual form, in terms of that fullness and clarity which corresponds in breadth to the unity of God. This will parallel the far-visioned goal of socialism to solve the material problems of humanity. Conventional theology assumes that the different religions must necessarily oppose each other, that each one must, by the very nature of its being, negate the other. In dealing with the moral issue of tolerance, it is constrained to invoke the concept of doubt and uncertainty in the realm of religion. In doing so it resembles the immaturity in the personal and national, the economic and social realms, which are in a state of opposition and competitiveness as long as human society is not yet fully developed."[4] Kook was aware that the psychic life force which is alive in mankind must become one with the cosmic life force which fills creation in its infinite multiplicity and possibilities. There can be no separation between the richness of life that is active in material life and the intellectual and imaginative forces active in spiritual life. The duality has meaning only for logical purposes that necessitate a division between the outer and the inner reality, the reality of the senses and that of the intellect. Life pulsates in all creation, all that bears the divine breadth, the richness of nature, the uniqueness of thinking.

Man can reach no unity with God, but he seeks through his thinking and his imagination to find those analogies which make the Idea of unity a possibility. "Unable to experience a direct and unmediated inner union with God, man seeks to discover a divine unity in the world through secondary media – the processes of thinking, observing, reasoning,

---

[4] "Fragments of Light: A View as to the Reasons for the Commandments," in *Abraham Isaac Kook*, 311.

through scholarly assumptions and hypotheses."[5] Bergman pointed to man's insatiable need to find a place for his reality with God. If God was not in all things, man sought to find the reality of all things in God. Knowing that such identity remains an impossibility at the present stage of human existence, man envisions the future as the redemptive hope, the time when the world will no longer be separated from God. This is the vision of the cosmic evolution, the optimism which carries mankind from generation to generation negating every enticement to be subject to a presence that is fixed and determined. There is development which implies a redemption of evil, a courage to defy the permanency of man's waywardness and destruction. There is an audacity in the belief that there is no evil and no death, but this audaciousness is inseparable from faith and hope. Bergman, like Rav Kook, knew that in courage religion and philosophy found the purpose of their journey in the world. If philosophy and religion do not prove their assumption they have learned to struggle for theirs; they have found other powers to affirm their truths, the inner convictions of the spirit.

Bergman's thought and faith remained firmly anchored in the conviction that evolution meant more than biological adaptation and struggle for survival. We could speak of an evolution of creation toward God, the yearning of the infinite multiplicity towards its creator, the living creative power which is the source of movement and love in every particle of creation. "The return of everything to its divine Source," Bergman stated, "is the completeness of the cosmic evolutionary process. Thus, Kook gives a cosmo-religious interpretation and endorsement to Darwin's theory of evolution which, in his judgment, comes closer to the spirit of Jewish mysticism than any other concept developed by modern science.... Unlike Darwin...Kook sees the moving force in the yearning of all that exists for the full discovery of God and for the return to Him."[6] We face a dynamic world of change and development where fixity and definition are only temporary phenomena. Time becomes cosmic, and the spatial and temporal quality of reality loses its apparent permanency and is transfigured by a new time and space in which phenomena lose their relativity and fleeting characteristic and depend upon man thinking "I" to give them categorical assurance and purpose. Man doesn't come to the rescue of chaotic phenomena with arbitrary plans of order; man finds the evolutionary process revealing a purpose and order that he didn't create or imagine. Man discovers that his "I" doesn't create reality, it describes the reality which was given from the Beginning.

---

[5]"Rav Kook: A Reality Is in God" in *Faith and Reason: An Introduction to Modern Jewish Thought* (New York, Schocken Books, 1963).
[6]*Ibid.*, 128.

Before Sinai, man received the Law. Unlike Kant and Idealism, man didn't find God in the inner moral law and then reveal it to himself. Man responded to the given Law and struggles to comprehend the Law in himself and in the Cosmos, the order created by God.

Nothing strikes us with greater astonishment than Kook's belief that evil as an autonomous power doesn't exist. Neither Bergman nor Kook were naive men. They lived in Palestine and Israel in their critical and crisis periods. Their perspectives make the difference between the man who is glued to reality and has identified it with truth, and the one whose time and space has become future, and who therefore deals with reality, but at the same time sees it as a passing phenomenon. Other truths are emerging from what is immediate and imposing upon our senses and thinking. We think of the reality that surrounds us and of the one that transcends existence. There are those rare individuals, those "princes of holiness," those "giants of faith" who offer us new visions and insights. We can think of any period in history, and we hear witnesses who reveal the ugliness and distortion that afflicts human nature, who reveal the devastating effects of war and demoralization, who turn either to the left or to the right in their attitudes and find hope in the magic of surrealism or those museums without walls. There are those who know the misery, look fully at the world, and, with a cosmic vision, believe everything to be good. They believe that "life is a constant process of growth toward perfection, a progression from less perfect to increasingly more perfect states of being.... Hence evil is not an intrinsic, inevitable aspect of life; it is man's unfinished task in the world. The function of this so-called evil is to push evolution ahead until men will realize the distinction between good and evil is unreal."[7]

Man's limited capacities to comprehend make it possible for him to conceive of evil either as a substantive reality or the inevitable source of human goodness. Man will always believe that evil is necessary for goodness, that the Heraclitian conflict of opposites is the source of human understanding. For God there is no evil. The later is a human creation. "In the same way," Bergman stated, "death for Kook is non-existent. According to the Biblical legend, Adam was punished for his sin of disobedience by becoming mortal. His sin brought death as well as man's fear of death into being. But the return of the world to its source will conquer death. Every improvement of the individual or the world, every act leading toward the achievement of perfection constitutes a step toward the conquest of death by the return of the world to its original state of union with God. Death is a lie; it is an illusion.... If sin brought death into being, *Teshuvah*, man's return to the

---

[7]*Ibid.*, 131.

Cosmic Faith

source of his being, will conquer it."[8] The question of death plays a decisive role in the thought of both Rav Kook and Hugo Bergman. It is the foundation of the philosophy of the belief in eternity. Man's soul is part of an eternal movement that returns again to its divine source at the time of bodily death; it always returns to God in *Teshuvah*, in penitence.

Bergman was not hesitant to put down the articles of his faith. In 1963, he put forth eight articles of faith. The third began with the words, "I do not believe in the reality and existence of death. Death, as Rav Kook said, is only an illusion, and because it is an illusion and a lie, it defiles. The consequence is that our life has a radically different meaning from what we are accustomed daily to believe. Only on *Yom Kippur* do we think differently. I state that man lives after death and must give an account for his life. In Isaiah it states, 'He shall eat the fruits of his works (Isa. 3:10).' I don't know and I make no philosophical assumption about what life is after death, but I am sure that life goes on and we must there give account for what we have done."[9]

Bergman's thoughts about *Teshuvah* evoke not only a personal experience but also a cosmic vision. The world seeks to realize the divine lights that live within it, to return them to the source of creation. Philosophy seeks to comprehend the depths of man's spiritual self, its growing powers to grasp the divine outflow that flows into creation, but the soul must turn towards God and struggle to be with him.

Rav Kook, in his *The Lights of Penitence* (Orot Hateshuvah, 1925), made us aware of how deeply he listened to the tradition as it flowed into him from the sages. "When we realize," he said, "to what extent the smallest particularities of existence, the spiritual and the material in miniature, all embody the general principles, and the smallest fragment has elements of greatness in the depths of its being, we shall no longer be surprised at the mystery of penitence that penetrates so deeply the spirit of man, that pervades him from the inception of this thought and world outlook to the minutest details of his acts and the expression of his character. The process is reenacted in the historical processes of humanity."[10] We need to discern "the luminous relationship between the great cosmic form of penitence in its broadest, deepest, and highest aspects and the penitence of the person, the individual and the collective, on whose orbit revolve all the strategies of the practical and spiritual life."[11]

---

[8]*Ibid.*, 132-133.
[9]*Tagebuecher*, 12/9/63.
[10]*The Lights of Penitence* in *Abraham Isaac Kook*, 81-82.
[11]*Ibid.*, 82.

In penitence man overcomes the fear of death. The latter loses its massive power, its name fades, and man finds the belonging to his people, to the world and the divine splendor that flows into the world. Penitence frees man from the fate of existence. The philosophers and literary men of post-World War I Europe indulge their imagination with human obituaries. We remember the novels of Drieu La Rochelle and of Céline, the philosophical investigations of Heidegger, and we turn with despair and weakness from the descriptions of human degeneracy and powerlessness. In a world rushing toward the consequences of the varied forms of totalitarianism, the voice of penitence and its cosmic consequence sought a place. The denial of evil and death were its greatest victories but these depended on man's moral conversion. "Penitence," Kook reminded us, "elevates the person and his world to that level where all existence stands in the clarity of its spiritual content. Penitence is the force through which man raises himself beyond limits of his needs and wishes. In penitence he is given a cosmic view of reality; he prepared himself for the 'new heaven' and 'new earth' which are already in creation. Penitence is the source of heroism, the power to move toward that unity of the lower and the higher divine essences,to overcome the fragmentations where 'every particular being stands by himself and evil is evil in and of itself, and it is evil and destructive.'"[12]

The cosmic quality of *Teshuvah* is inseparable from the belief in constant renewal. *Teshuvah* is not simply a return, but it is an enlightenment, "the perception that dawns on a person to see the world not as finished, but as in the process of continued becoming, ascending, developing – this changes him from being 'under the sun' to being 'above the sun,' from the place where there is nothing new to the place where there is nothing old, where everything takes on a new form. The joy of heaven and earth abides in him as on the day they were created. In this luminous perspective one looks at all the worlds, at the general and the human development, at the destiny of each creature, at all the events of all times."[13]

Bergman sought a cosmic view in which mankind found a unique place and a distinct mission. The works of Rav Kook remained influential throughout his life. No problem is more baffling for philosophy than death and immortality. They demanded new concepts of time and place, a constant spiritual regeneration both of man and the universe. Philosophy reassumed a faith in immortality that few other human activities dared to face and from which most philosophers retreated. Bergman remained loyal, intimately involved in these cosmic

---

[12]*Ibid.*, 85.
[13]"Lights of Holiness" in *Abraham Isaac Kook*, 229.

speculations. He was struck and awed by them; they captured his soul and he knew that it was his destiny to follow his faith.

There are no extensive references to Pierre Teilhard de Chardin in Bergman's *Diaries*, but there are entries that he read Teilhard and wrote an article review on him. What is significant is the closeness of the ideas that Teilhard enunciated and those which were at the core of Bergman's philosophy. In 1961, Bergman spoke of his reading of Teilhard and of his article in the Hebrew Encyclopedia. Previously, he reviewed the German edition of the *Phenomenon of Man* and had written of the relationship between Rav Kook and Teilhard.[14] Each believer was attached to a religious tradition, found it necessary to justify that tradition within the dimensions of his thinking, but the scope and depth of Kook's and Teilhard's thinking surpassed the faiths from which they emerged. The same problem confronted Bergman. These men had a sense of the religious and they are joined by many others who have attempted to bring together the principles of their faith and the depths of their inspirations. They were men of veiled worlds and what they said in one constantly revealed another. Their books are sources for books, and the paths which they mark out are always inadequate and inconvenient for those who know that for them truths lie behind truths, and that we are traveling in directions that are greater than the signs given by their authors. Those who surround them feel the shaking of the foundations and are fearful. These men make others uncomfortable and unhappy and for this reason much of their effort becomes apologetical. To survive, they must placate their disclaimers, for they too have truths.

In the *Divine Milieu* (1926), Teilhard spoke autobiographically. He said that "the man with a passionate sense of the divine *milieu* cannot bear to find things about him obscure, tepid and empty when it should be full and vibrant with God. He is paralyzed by the thought of the numberless spirits which are linked to his in the unity of the same world, but are not yet fully kindled by the flame of the divine presence. He had thought for a time that he had only to stretch out his *own* in order to touch God to the measure of his desires. He now sees that the only human embrace capable of worthily enfolding the divine, is that of all men opening their arms to call down and welcome the Fire. The only subject ultimately capable of mystical transfiguration is the whole group of mankind forming a single body and a single soul in charity."[15]

The community of mankind is more than a depository of convictions, i.e., the protector of traditional faith and individuals, but it bears witness

---

[14]*The Writings of Shmuel Hugo Bergman: A Bibliography*, 1903-1967 (Jerusalem), The Magnes Press, 1968.
[15]*The Divine Milieu* (New York, Harper Torch Books, 1965), 144.

to the future, to the mankind that is yet to come into existence and whose relationship to God will deepen our awareness of how intimately man is dependent upon the divine for the realization of his being. Man not only confesses a faith; he assumes the task of being its bearer. Teilhard, like Bergman and Kook, knew that the awe of religious faith belonged to the witnessing of new spiritual dimensions, of a new qualitative partnership between mankind and God. Mankind had a cosmic role to play in the receptivity of God's love, and the movement towards a cosmic mankind. The power of response revealed the longing that lay in the human reality, and above all, in a mankind being moved towards God.

Teilhard spoke of the opposition between an open and a closed world. Man was breaking through the spiritual and traditional limitations that enclosed his science and his politics. He speaks of global economics that joins continents and nations into areas of cooperation and dependence and makes us aware that we can leap political boundaries when new forms of union become viable and meaningful. Nations don't dissolve, but their interrelationships take on new dimensions and forms, which previously would have been thought to be inconceivable. Global economics transforms political life. Nations depend upon nations, and independence is interdependence. Teilhard's visions broke through the beliefs in biological and mechanical progress. They assumed cosmic dimensions, and with these new forms, religion had to adjust the traditions, but the latter were not always universal. Men had made them identical with a new reality of time and space. "It is becoming increasingly difficult," Teilhard stated, "for a true science of man (that is to say, 'an anthropology of movement'), not to make a choice between two terms of this dilemma which is still left to professional metaphysicians and moralists. *And the reason for this is* that from the moment when man recognizes that he is in a state of evolution, he can no longer progress unless he develops in himself a deep-rooted, passionate zest for his own evolution; and there is the further reason for it is precisely this dynamic zest that could be vitiated beyond repair and annihilated by the prospect, however far ahead it may be, of a definitive and total death. No; if the world is not automatically to destroy its own dynamic drive in step with its hominization, it cannot be of the 'closed' type."[16]

Teilhard made us aware that he was not simply talking about the movement of energies from above and from below. He didn't have before him a law of the universe from which he described the nature of creation. There is more than one type of energy. Teilhard spoke of an

---

[16]"The Activation of Human Energy" unpublished 1953 in *Activation of Energy* (New York, Harcourt Brace Jovanovich, 1970), 391-392.

axial energy that is "increasing and irreversible" and a peripheral or tangential one that is "constant and reversible." These types of energy operate on different levels; they are not transformed into each other. We are speaking of varied movements of energies which refused to be explained causally. We realize that the different types of energy correspond to the varied ways that the divine permeates the world that surrounds us. No longer is it easy to define the relationship of divinity to universal life by one or another movement. We are aware that matter is no longer comprehensible as the prison of the soul, as a force that should be overcome and transfigured. Matter bears within it the divine imprint. It is filled with divine "lights," but their energies transcend the simplistic directions of above and below. The multiple energies that dwell in matter and constitute its reality have only just begun to make man aware that living in him, and in nature, there are infinite sources of energy that cannot be differentiated. In other words, the dualisms that have become a part of the religious vocabulary no longer make it possible for us to see all things in God. In this vision, in this pantheism, we find that we encompass a dynamism between God and man that harbors new dreams and visions of development and change.

The vision that ties Teilhard to Bergman and to Kook, is that "little by little, stage by stage." Teilhard said, "everything is finally linked to the supreme center in *quo omnia constant.* The streams which flow from this center operate not only within the higher reaches of the world, where human activities take place in a distinctively supernatural and meritorious form. In order to save and establish these sublime forces, the power of the Word Incarnate penetrates matter itself; it goes down into the deepest depths of the lower forces."[17] We live not only with mechanical laws that govern causal change, but we live with future expectations and it is the religious quality of life that gives scope and drama to these hopes. We feel the power of transcendence and transfiguration. Kook spoke of the land and air of Israel as if they had transfigurative powers, sacramental qualities. When we are so deeply attached to a romantic vision that finds its concreteness in the immediacies of existence, we easily find the way to skepticism and fantasy. Bergman's Zionism, as the sanctification of the Holy Name, brought with it a political and moral burden that far surpassed the capacity of the Jewish settlers in Palestine and Israel. Teilhard's concept of a Cosmic Eucharist presupposed man's capacities for faith and imagination to be greater than they have been hitherto. The visions and hopes remain the life of the spirit, but man's cultural and moral development lies far behind in potentiality.

---

[17]*The Divine Milieu,* 61-62.

At an international philosophical congress held in Jerusalem in 1965, Bergman addressed the delegates. He told the audience of his experience at the Fourth International Congress that was held in Bologna in 1911. The coming of the war seemed to be a reality and the philosophers met to determine if there was anything they could do to prevent it. Henri Bergson was the speaker, but a German philosopher had to be elected president of the session. "Three years later," Bergman noted, "the conflict came and we philosophers went, like all the others, with a Hurrah to the war. I was among them. I must admit, when I think of it, that the generation of 1914 and that of 1939 were unprepared – I mean unprepared not only politically, but morally and spiritually. I have grave doubts about the task which philosophers fulfill today in human society."[18]

We know that Bergman's lifelong search was to find a way by which the philosopher could show mankind its purpose and its meaning. Bergman sought discussion with believers from the West and of the East. He turned often to Sri Aurobindo, to the theosophist Rudolf Steiner, to his colleague Martin Buber, and those many others whose thoughts involved new visions, courage, and hopes for mankind. The question Bergman raised before the Congress was, "What should we do? At first we must pose to ourselves the question: Can we change the human species and if we can, in what directions?"[19]

Bergman's thought was never separated from Messianism. He believed that a radical change had to take place in man's moral situation before we could expect any change in the human situation. He told the delegates that he was sure of one thing: man as he is today, made from crooked wood, as Kant said, is not capable of resolving the problems that his one-sided technical-intellectual accomplishments have brought forth. If man does not change, he will be destroyed. Nature will perhaps find a way to resolve the problem and change the *Homo Sapiens* (the knowing man, as he calls himself), and create anew man: an 'Overman.' If we use this word, then it is not in the Nietzschean sense, but in the meaning of the Messianic expectation of Judaism, Christianity, and of the Indian wise men.... If today we discuss the 'Understanding of history,' let us not forget that it is not obvious that history will go forth."[20]

Bergman entitled his remarks, "The Responsibility of Philosophers." This is a theme which men must consider as the perpetual problem of man's future. The philosophers have a particular duty to address the problem again and again. The philosopher is naturally tied to societal,

---

[18]*Mitteilungsblatt*, June 4, 1965.
[19]*Ibid.*
[20]*Ibid.*

national and universal problems. He is the man without a designated spiritual homeland; his responsibility is to mankind. Knowing that every man belongs to a tradition, a language, and a culture forces him to build bridges to as many other traditions and cultures as is possible. Man builds perspectives, visions of a universal mission that enhances and deepens man's sense of humanity and its divine source. The Messianic expectations of Judaism, Christianity, and the wisdom of Indian thinkers like Sri Aurobindo, need to become living reality among men. How we find our way to the future depends on the way we find to the sources of our faith and reason. Sri Aurobindo spoke of this subliminal change when he said that "the state of the being after this supramental transformation, will be in all the parts of consciousness and knowledge that of an infinite and cosmic consciousness acting through the universalized individual Puruska (soul). The fundamental power will be an awareness of identity, a knowledge by identity – an identity of being, of consciousness, of force of being and consciousness, of delight of being, an identity with the Infinite, the Divine and with all that is in the Infinite, all that is the expression and manifestation of the Divine."[21]

Bergman sought in these spiritual expressions new dimensions of spiritual life. Man endeavors to find these expressions link religion to philosophy. Philosophy is a religious struggle with its own tools and instruments. It is rooted in the eternal quest for transcendence, for ever-new horizons of man's imagination and hope. The intimacy of the human-divine partnership has essential reality for Bergman's thought, but it was the Idea of cosmic evolution, the yearning of all things for their source, that became the primal reality of his faith. He believed, like Rav Kook, that the strength of the soul is in prayer. He quoted Kook's belief that *everything* prays and that "Prayer is the ideal of all worlds. All of existence longs for the source of its life. Each plant and bush, each grain of sand, and clod of earth, everything in which life is revealed, everything in which life is hidden, all of the smaller works of Creation and all of the larger ones, the skies above and the holy angels, all the minute details in all of existence, as well as its totality, *everything* yearns, strives, pines and longs for the delight of the perfection of its High Source, living, holy, pure and mighty."[22]

Teilhard took his place among those creative and courageous men who refused to shy away from the powers of their imagination and the consequences of their work and meditation. Teilhard spoke of "The

---

[21]*The Synthesis of Yoga* (Pondicherry, Sri Aurobindo Ashram, 1988), 851-852.
[22]"Prayer in the Thought of Rav Kook," *Conservative Judaism*, Vol. 20, No. 4. Summer 1966. See: *Essays on the Thought and Philosophy of Rabbe Kook* (Herzl Press, 1991), 70.

Religion of Tomorrow." He said that "although we are not as alive to it as we should be, the key question that is beginning to present itself to Mankind in process of planetary arrangement, is a problem of spiritual *activation* – new powers call for new aspirations. If Mankind is to use its new access to physical power (Atomic power) with balanced control, it cannot do without a rebound of intensity in the eagerness to act, to seek, to create."[23] These remarks belong to the last words that Teilhard wrote. They came forth as the consequences of what he thought and fought to make real to his colleagues and the world. He set forth the Idea that man needs a Religion of Evolution "ever more explicitly if he is to survive and to 'super-live' as soon as he becomes conscious of his power to ultra-hominize himself and of his duty to do so. *In a system of cosmo-noogenesis, the comparative value of a religious creed may be measured by their respective power of evolutive activation.*"[24] From these remarks emerge Teilhard's question about the religion of tomorrow and the source of its thought in the philosophy and theology of today. It comes forth from a thinking that dominates our world, and is yet not too radical for those who live with traditional reality. The reality is embracing and challenging; it forces us to believe.

Teilhard feared little the criticism of contemporary religions and he made it very clear that "religions are still systematically closed to the wide horizons and great winds of cosmogenesis, and can no longer truly be said to feel with the Earth – an Earth whose internal frictions they can lubricate like a soothing oil, but whose driving energies they cannot animate as they should."[25] There is a sense of loneliness in his voice, the despair of man who knows that there are few with whom he can share his vision and even fewer who will dare to embrace his ideas. There is little comfort in knowing that other men in other places and at other times have had similar experiences. Ideas that don't join their time become threatening and abrasive, and men resist their presence with scorn and suspicion. "How, most of all, can it be," stated Teilhard, "that 'when I come down from the mountain' and in spite of the glorious vision I still retain, I find that I am so little a better man, so little at peace, so incapable of expressing in my actions, and thus adequately communicating to others the wonderful unity that I feel encompassing me?"[26]

---

[23]"The Christic" in *The Heart of the Matter* (San Diego, Harcourt Brace Jovanovich, 1978), 96.
[24]*Ibid.*, 97.
[25]*Ibid.*, 98.
[26]*Ibid.*, 100.

There is in Teilhard that precious loneliness of soul that knows that there is almost no one with whom he can share the wonders that he has seen, nor is there comfort in the works of others because no one has had a similar vision. But, then, there are men, multitudes, who are potentially capable of understanding what Teilhard had described. "It is indeed heartening," he said, "to know that I am not a lone discoverer, but that I am, quite simply, responding to the vibration that is necessarily active in all the souls around me. It is, in consequence, exhilarating to feel that I am not just myself or all alone, that my name is legion and that I am 'all men.'"[27]

There are two anchors of faith; one that draws us toward the love of God and the other that adheres to the belief in the world. So easily we have torn them apart and with so much difficulty we attempt to bring them together. The moment we put aside our disdain for matter, and with awe become aware of the creative process within it, we become aware that the lights of the divine are as present in it as they are in the spirit. Israel declared with fervent conviction the Oneness of God and with these words her faithful often went to their death. We have a similar truth to affirm with our belief in the goodness of creation and sacredness of matter. The Oneness flows to all things as it flows from them to God. Teilhard said, a month before his death, that "this is one more proof that Truth has to appear only once, in one single mind, for it to be impossible for anything ever to prevent it from spreading universally and setting everything ablaze."[28]

We read the works of Teilhard and we have the distinct feeling that he always loved the world and his belief in the immortality of the spirit was divine grace. Deeply embedded in this spirit and love is the cosmic universalism that was sacred to Hugo Bergman. Teilhard spoke of the "Eastern, human and Christian" currents slowing finding a single voice "in which a religion of the future can be conceived." Bergman was opposed to any religious exclusivity; he felt disturbed with the Christocentric vocabulary of Teilhard, but he knew that behind the traditional language lived a higher truth that encompassed language, ritual and articles of faith. His philosophy emerged from penitence, and the sanctification of the Holy Name. He stated in 1967 that "God saved our small state and thus gave us the possibility for the sanctification of His Name in this state. It can become the heart of humanity, not through power nor through strength, but only through His Spirit."[29]

---

[27]*Ibid.*, 101.
[28]*Ibid.*, 102.
[29]*Tagebuecher*, 8/21/67.

We wonder at the miracle that will make the state the receptacle for the Holy Spirit; we wonder at sacredness of land and air, at evolution and the oneness of soul and body, but we cannot deny that the wonders of the imagination reveal the ever-present divinity that dwells within us.

Bergman had many spiritual companions but he was never a disciple. He was a believer. The contents of his faith developed as his vision and hope grew in clarity and intimacy. He belonged to world and spirit but in each he was a man on a journey drawn by the Divine to the lands of the unknown. These were the Promised Lands.

6

Messianic Faith

In Bergman's *Diaries and Letters*, there is a letter from the philosopher to one of his closest and distinguished students, Jacob Fleischmann. Fleischmann died recently in Paris. He was recognized as one of Europe's leading scholars of Hegel, the author of a distinguished and novel book on Jewish-Christian relations, *Christianisme à nu (Christianity Laid Bare)*. Bergman's letter is a reply to a letter of Fleischmann, and reveals more cogently and profoundly his attitude to philosophy and religion than any other single document. For this reason, I believe that it deserves a careful reading and commentary. Two years earlier, the year of his sixtieth birthday, Bergman stated the articles of his faith. When he finished his statement, he told a parable, "I said to the man who stood at the gate of the year: Give me a light that I may tread safely into the unknown. And he replied: Go out into the darkness, and put your hand into God's hand. That shall be to you better than light and safer than a known way.[1]

We ask if learning is possible without faith and we believe that faith belongs both to the human spirit and to God's will. We believe that there is no learning without faith or that learning creates its own faith. Bergman was certain that faith precedes learning, guides and orders it, but he never believed that it hinders and does violence to it. We will understand more fully the relationship between learning and faith as we read through the letter and attempt to grasp the meaning of the articles of faith. We know that learning can never be without faith and faith is empty without learning. If we speak of Bergman as a believing philosopher, we have difficulties and contradictions. Is not a believing philosopher a contradiction or is he a being who is deeply aware of the power that contradictions exercise on each other? In fact, what

---

[1] *Tagebuecher & Briefe*, 12/28/43.

characterized Bergman's uniqueness was his capacity to move from thinker to thinker and realize in this movement the force and impetus that ideas – even opposite ideas – have upon each other. It is the relationship of opposites, the "coincidence of opposites" that constitutes the essence of his philosophical and theological thought.

Bergman stated clearly in his letter that he didn't believe that the philosopher or philosophy should be tied to national or local conditions or that we should suppose that these conditions are fundamental for the understanding of either the philosopher or philosophy. Bergman remarked, "I do not see Kant as a German, nor Plato as a Greek. Naturally, the greatest man is born in a certain milieu and is influenced by it. I do not believe that Kant was 'rooted in his people' to the degree that the passage from his theoretical philosophy to reality was achieved with fewer conflicts by a German Kant-student, than the corresponding passage with a Jewish or Italian Kant-student. In fact, there are few great philosophers and they extend their hands to each other and form a chain which goes beyond people and homeland. "Philosophy is rooted in depths which are beyond Germanness or Jewishness or Greekness."[2]

The philosopher also walks in the public arena and faces the problems that he finds in it. Bergman was always in that arena with his colleagues Martin Buber, Gershom Scholem, Nathan Rotenstreich, and Ernst Simon. They were thinkers in a land on the verge of independence, attempting to find solutions for inherent national conflicts which created violent problems between Jews and Arabs. These men were not incarcerated in lecture halls, but molders of public opinion. They were creators of public opinion in and outside of them. They walked the streets of many cities and spoke to many audiences and were brutally aware of how deep went their responsibilities to the vision and hope that would be Israel, a nation not only among nations, but a model of justice where justice had never been. Listening to Bergman's words and hearing their universality, we find courage and hope in their universalism. They were surrounded by the sharpness of nationalism that had emerged from the retreat of the imperial powers, and had its origins in nineteenth century Europe. Men sought belonging to lands and peoples to histories and religions and Bergman knew this well from his native city of Prague. He was a child of Prague, an admirer of Thomas Masaryk, first president of Czechoslovakia, whose sympathy with nationalism was very limited. Bergman recalled some concluding words about him given in Jerusalem in 1941. "We do know from where he looks down upon us, upon the children of his people, who together

---

[2] *Ibid.*, 9/6/45.

with the children of Israel, the Poles and the southern Slavs have been united here (in Palestine)."[3]

Bergman noted that the great man creates from and beyond the national level and "for this reason he belongs to the family of mankind and if you say that philosophy is the stuff (*Sache* 'wirklicher' Philosophen) of the real philosophers who do not live in a world of generality, I answer negatively: ...they are great philosophers because their reality is generality, and their generality is reality. Their generality is so strong, that it is not a pale-abstractness, but actuality."[4]

We venture to think of the ideas that moved Bergman's thought. He lived with universality, with the ethical visions of the prophets. He quoted often the fourth chapter of Zechariah, "Not by might, nor by power, but by My spirit – said the Lord of Hosts,"[5] but his deepest insight was the *complexio oppositorum*, his awareness of the spirit that found the depths of its reality in movement from one moment of thought to another. These movements lived from their opposites which made it possible to explore with fullness and perplexity, sympathy and comprehension, the thought of a philosopher, to discover within it the need and power to move away from it, and to seek in the opposite, strength and profundity. We could speak of the correlation of opposites, and inner tension in thinking which denies to any moment of thinking autonomy and absoluteness and reveals the depths of dependence and receptivity which thought recognizes in thought.

Bergman observed that "the more minor a philosopher is, the more consequence will a philosophical anthropology yield for the understanding of his philosophy. He does not belong to that chain of great brothers who are beyond time and place and who continue among themselves their conversation, Plato and Kant, etc., beyond the events of history and geography."[6] Philosophy is a universal task reaching out beyond the continents of thinkers who know that they belong to a community of beings who believe in the power of the spirit, and who remain loyal to Kant's faith that what man can do depends upon what he should do. Bergman was the culmination of a line of thinkers from Hermann Cohen to Franz Rosenzweig to Martin Buber. But he not only stood with them, he went beyond them in his comprehension of the coincidence of opposites and the concept of a "Believing Community." He sought to reach the thought of India through his closeness and devotion to Sri Aurobindo, whose Ashram he visited in 1947. There is an

---
[3]*Ibid.*, 9/14/41.
[4]*Ibid.*, 8/6/45.
[5]*Tanakh* (Philadelphia, Jewish Publication Society, 1985).
[6]*Tagebuecher*, 8/6/43.

extraordinary sense of universal sympathy in Bergman which can be continuously comprehended in his *Diaries and Letters*. His was a vision dialoguing ideas that moved through time and space. We have no system, but a foundation and an embrace that fascinates the mind and, at times, stuns the imagination. We wonder how such a vision is created and we are forced to surrender to our inadequacies. Bergman, unlike Hegel or Kant, creates no system of thought which we can study in detail. He leads us on an adventure, but he takes us only a few steps and then sets us free to travel alone. We either return to our studies, or we venture further, guided only by the light of the idea and the courage of the imagination. However, we go there as a spiritual guide that Bergman gives us. He remarked about himself, "I cannot identify myself with something that is not my life only to have ground under my feet."[7] Each of us must know where we must search for the truth of our being, and the spiritual dwelling in which we find strength.

Bergman mentioned that in Fleischmann's letter there is a second issue which is ultimately tied to the first. This is the problem of religion. Bergman remarks that "here my position is less certain. In your letter I see two questions: 1. belief and philosophy, 2. belief and Judaism."[8] These are the constant problems which find no final answers. Men discover that there are particular and distinct experiences which defy general and universal definitions. We move from faith to reason, from form to freedom, from unity to multiplicity and we find in neither one nor the other answers that satisfy either need or spirit. Bergman, more than any other philosopher, moves spiritually through the world of ideas. He was capable of expounding a system of thought with remarkable consistency and conviction, and then move to another opposite in value, with equal strength and devotion. Was this a remarkable ability or an indecisiveness which weakened the image which others demanded of him? Decisiveness and the fervor of orthodoxy satisfies more readily those who need a figure to follow and phrases to repeat. Bergman would give neither. His thought rested in a fundamental belief in the spirit, a faith in its efficacy and an appreciation of its beauty; but the expressions and images, inspirations and intimacies of the spirit found little rest in one mode or another of his life. In Bergman, love was rich and efficacious, and like the origin of love in Plato's *Symposium,* its poverty was an *absence,* and it saw in every metaphor and allegory only a step toward a higher spiritual life and direction. Bergman, different from most of his contemporaries, found no rest in one or another path, in one or another dream and hope. In

---

[7] *Ibid.*, 10/1/64.
[8] *Ibid.*, 8/6/45.

monotheism, in the uniqueness of God, he discovered truth and goodness.

With this metaphysical disquietude, Bergman attempted to reveal the sufferings of the lover in whom philosophy had found a demon. In the simplicity of his physical existence, he harbored a whirlwind which knew no fortress nor haven of rest. Those who surrounded him were aware that they were always on a journey, and like St. Augustine, he was a pilgrim who in the present never lost the power of the future. He wrote in his letter that he agreed with Fleischmann when he says that philosophy is not the effective means to awaken religious feelings. Its function is more negative than positive. It resolves 'a few doubts,' it can for modern man free the way to faith. It can, for example, through philosophical means resolve the question: Is it permitted to pray? "That would, however, not bring man to clasp his hands, but it might make it possible for him to do it."[9]

We may be liberated by philosophy to approach the religious commitment and act, but philosophy does not make it possible for us to do it. The transition, "the leap," is beyond our will; it lies in a power over which we have no control and where will is not our will, where love is not our love. Religion bears within it a mystery which defies our definitions and explanations. With philosophy, we explain and ignore what exists; with faith we have to come to terms with what has been divinely given to us. We need a new order of experience and a new language of images and metaphors. Philosophy may go towards religion, but religion is not its creation nor the consequence of its formulations. Religion begins with the two mystical words: I believe, and it struggles with them through the life of the believer. Philosophy satisfies its task when it shows man the little pomegranate seed. "Hegel," Bergman noted, "wanted to establish the highest religion on pure thought, but in this he erred. He failed to understand that the immediate and experientially limited character of religion is experienced and not thought."[10]

The critique of Hegel applies also to Hermann Cohen, who could not free religion from philosophy, who could not make that leap of faith which gives religion its uniqueness and the power of its expression. Bergman made that passage, but stood in both realms, which, at times, appeared contradictory, but beyond appearances there was the unyielding faith and a highly developed sense of reasoning. They belonged to each other in the peculiar synthesis which is every man's distinct experience. The correlation of these two experiences made it

---

[9] *Ibid.*
[10] *Ibid.*

impossible to think of their unity or identity. Their belonging was both spiritual and physical; they belonged not only to speculation but to the everyday living of the spirit, to the conversation, to writing, to teaching and public involvement. Philosophy and religion became mutual and contradictory ways for the believing philosopher.

Bergman did not find it difficult to discuss the relationship between religion and Judaism. This touched the soul of the philosopher in a very peculiar way. He was drawn to his own confession, to the daily habits and values, but he knew a broader picture that necessitated the place of his historic faith in relation to those of others, to Christianity, to Islam, to Hinduism and to Buddhism. Bergman remarked, "I don't believe in an absolute religion. All religions are, in my eyes, methods to a goal. The dogmatic distinctions are artistic superstructures which religions have built either over or under their edifice, and they are, in my view, not important. Since the methods are, for the most part, pedagogical, they must consider the souls of people and the epoch to which they speak."[11] Bergman's position seems at first difficult to comprehend. He was a practicing Jew, deeply devoted to tradition and a student of Jewish thought, Talmudic and philosophical and speculative. In fact, there was little that did not interest him. Judaism, we may say, was his way; a way he had inherited and believed to be meaningful and purposeful, not only for Israel, but for all mankind. But this attitude he applied to other faiths and religious thinkers. Each faith bears within it a divine seed that develops in its history and literature; each confers its uniqueness upon itself, and its truth and beauty flows to all faiths. Bergman was a listening philosopher, like the ancient Pythagoreans, and when he thought he was listening, words carried vast and precious meanings for him and he taught those around him to find in words not only their apparent signs, but the symbolic paths they set in motion. From the truth of his way, he prepared himself for the truths that lay hidden in the ways of others. His method was an unveiling of truths that were buried in the phenomena we study and seek to comprehend.

His letter to Fleischmann continued, "For this reason Moses spoke in a different language than Jesus. Every people has its way to God and so does every epoch. God, however, is One, and if we feel a closeness to the Jewish tradition, it is because this pedagogy is close to our hearts – not the dogma. I do not believe in a particular mission of the Jewish people which we have witnessed so frightfully in our time. Therefore, it seems to me so vulgar and foolish when Zionism draws only political consequences from a religious-historical event."[12]

---

[11]*Ibid.*
[12]*Ibid.*

With these words, Bergman concluded his letter, and with characteristic humility, he tells Fleischmann that he knows his statements will be unsatisfactory and that he "sits between all the chairs (ich sitze zwischen allen Sesseln)."[13] In this humility, there is a profound truth. The human spirit may lodge itself in one faith or another and emerge from its dwelling with more and more strength, but it also feels a longing for a new pilgrimage at the same time. Bergman wandered from one spiritual land to the next, seeking in each what divinity had implanted in it. He moved from Prague to Jerusalem and from there to the world of Sri Aurobindo and then he traveled to the world of Rudolf Steiner, to Frithjof Schuon, to René Guénon to meditations on Romano Guardini and Georg Picht. He lived with the mood and reality created by a prayer of atonement: "Read, read – live? serving God?" He knew there could be no end to learning, no end to questions about the meaning of life and no desire to cease the struggle for service to God. With no absolute truth, but only journeys into a world where there could be no absolute dwelling, this wandering philosopher had many spiritual homes. There was, however, the one home called Israel from which the journeys began and to which he returned. In that Jerusalem home, he gathered his strength and served his God. Fortified in his own tradition and confident of their truth, he could move to wherever a seed of truth called him. Of one thing he was absolutely certain, there could not be only a political Zion without religious vision and testimony. The call of the future rested in the faith that the God of Israel had a particular message for his people, a Messianic calling.

In 1943, Bergman was sixty. A deputation of students from the university, headed by Ostropolski and Fleischmann, brought him the gifts of the students. Bergman returned their greetings and gifts with a statement of faith. For Bergman, there was no separation between the personal and the public, between the man and the professor. Philosophy was too intimate an exploration and commitment to preserve such distinctions. In Bergman, the man and the philosopher were one, the believer and the thinker joined in one being. Philosophy came forth from the believer and the latter emerged through the philosopher. Thinking and believing sought, in the individual, for expression. Neither one nor the other sought definitions but rather living experiences. Neither one nor the other wanted domination. They learned from each other, and as they turned to the world around and beyond them, they sought clarification and comprehension. Each, like in Augustine's *Confessions* or Pascal's *Pensées*, revealed the paths of their development, their interrelationship and their parting of ways. They did not long for

---

[13]*Ibid.*

identification, nor even harmony. They were like different songs in the same soul. They knew that they needed each other in correlation, as freedom needs form, as reason needs prayer.

Bergman begins his confession of faith with the affirmation "that God is, has created the Heavens and the Earth. Only from our perspective, not from what He is in Himself, can we understand Him. God has created the world incomplete, to be completed. Time has reality. 'World Time,' *Die Weltstunde,* has reality. True time is more the physical."[14] Every beginning is a foundation from which everything else proceeds. Everything depends upon the beginning. We do not create this beginning; we find it and recognize it, affirm it and go forth from it. There is no thinking that doesn't proceed from a beginning, an assumption, an act of faith. Reason begins in an act of faith, in a self-affirmation and in giving a foundation. The heavens and the earth are set in relationship to God and to man. However, they formed what is significant in their belonging to those who declare them to be earth and heaven and give meaning to their reality. The creation is incomplete. Man must not only learn the laws of its existence; he must take responsibility for it. He learns that he is capable of knowledge, and moral behavior, but he is not a creator, but a co-creator. He presumes a partnership for himself with God, knowing that this is not a relationship of equals. From man's perspective, the creation is a challenge to his intelligence and ethics. He never forgets that what he does and thinks is derived from *his* perspective, from the reason that was born in him. God is not an object of knowledge; he is never grasped or comprehended by reason. God is both in and beyond the power of our language, the analogies, metaphors, allegories and images which we are necessitated to use when we speak of him. Beyond all these linguistic forms is man's secret weapon: the language of prayer.

Bergman now turned to the creation of man. He states "that God created man as a creator; that he limited his own freedom for the sake of man. That man in all his freedom is not abandoned by God, but permanently bound to him."[15] Human freedom is divine contradiction. The freedom which man is aware of has its source in the reality of choice. In God's self-limitation, man becomes aware of his freedom. Freedom is his because he has appropriated it from God. His freedom is the recognition of the image of the divinity within him. His freedom binds him to God and makes him responsible for the creation. Man is correlation with God in the realization of his freedom. I am free because God *is*. His being is in me freedom. The relationship between man and

---

[14]*Ibid.,* 12/20/43.
[15]*Ibid.*

God is for Bergman the foundation for the future of mankind. He found it impossible to think of man without God, and God without man. From his perspective ... *complexio oppositorum* is fundamental to all thinking. What is inexplicable, and yet awesome about thinking, is the relationship between antinomian laws which are dependent upon each other, and the source of vitality and truth for each other. Bergman is a thinker for whom opposites are the vital sources of the freedom that is man's uniqueness.

From man, Bergman turned to Israel, the path of a truth he followed throughout his life and which, at the same time, opened to him the other philosophical and religious paths which occupied his life. "I believe that God has chosen Israel. This is no mechanical chosenness, but all action between God and man occurs in correlation, i.e., in the freedom of man. That God chooses us depends always upon us. It is no mechanical treaty which obligates and bends God, but one which must be renewed every hour and particularly by us."[16] The power of Bergman's universalism lies in the correlation between the particular and the universal. His thought moves in both directions at the same time; the deeper his sense of particular belonging and obligation, the deeper his awareness that from every great religious source there is a universal message and correlation. Since everything in Bergman's thinking lies in that mystery of the "coincidence of opposites," we realize that every thought already implies another, every movement, its counter-movement, every image brings forth another. We are involved in a world of analogy. What is so very difficult in this type of thinking is the lack of security or absoluteness that rests in devotion to a system, or to a claim of absolute truth. The inner dissatisfaction, anxiety, and disruption can only be endured by the believing philosopher, and he faces the pain of the tension that draws thinking from one level of reality to another, from the attachment to tradition and history, the public marketplace and responsibility to our fellow citizen, to the symbolic world of future hopes and visions.

Bergman believed that Israel in that dualness of correlation and deed, needing to receive and through receiving to do, has become the instrument of God, through the chain of prophets to Jesus, all of whom saw the calling of Israel in this instrumentality, "It is too little that you should be my servant in that I raise up the tribes of Jacob and restore the survivors of Israel. I will also make you a light of nations that my salvation may reach the ends of the earth"[17] (Isaiah 49:6).

---

[16]*Ibid.*
[17]*Ibid.*

Bergman never surrendered the Messianic mission of Israel, a mission that must be radically separated from political Messianism created in the French Revolution. Israel's mission is given to her by God in service to mankind. This mission is revealed by the prophets and Jesus; it is the mission of monotheism. From this message which Israel has for mankind, comes the responsibility she has toward herself. She must comprehend the quality of life that she lives, and her attitude toward other peoples and faiths must be constantly valued and placed within the universal ethical demands of monotheism. Bergman stated, "that the generation which most deeply understood this mission was that of the young Jesus, and that at the moment, when this mission 'to the ends of the earth' became reality, it was mixed with myth from and with Pauline theology which made men simple tools and deprived them of freedom. Then the tragic moment entered our history, a greater misfortune than the destruction of the Holy Temple. The mission was taken from our hands and we gave it away. We were now concerned only with the one reality: to maintain ourselves, to withdraw into a snail shell. From that moment begins the battle of the two movements in which the prophetic movement is buried. Zionism developed from two conflicting movements: to preserve us and to renew us."[18]

In these words we are faced with a philosophy and theology of history that excites the imagination and challenges the reason. All the conflicts and struggles that have consumed the struggle between Judaism and Christianity, have their origins in Bergman's descriptions. Again and again we have sought to understand the relationship between Jesus and Israel, between Paul and the mission of Israel with the consequences that have befallen Israel: to live with two directions in her heart. Never could Israel escape the consequence of the Paulinian heritage: Augustine's vision of the Two Cities. Israel became only an historical moment of the conflict between these two cities, an important but finished section of a history that began with Adam and will end with the Second Coming of Christ. In other words, Israel has no longer a part to play in world history; she has played her role and is now a "fossil," a simple remains.

Bergman knew that Zionism should be more than a movement of self-preservation, the creation of a state among states. Israel's mission was not fully absorbed in the history of the Two Cities, nor was it subsumed in a political reality. Zionism remained embodied in Israel's vision and charge. From Israel there must emerge again the "Believing Community," a sense of openness and discourse which struggles to bring forth that communication among faiths and philosophers that sets aside

---

[18]*Ibid.*

absolute truths, but affirms the oneness of God. The spirit of Bergman's universalism was carried by many of his followers and friends. In the work of the great Israeli New Testament scholar David Flusser, Bergman found an intimate and close companion. In his book *Die rabbinischen Gleichnisse und der Gleichniserzaehler Jesus (Rabbinic Parables and Jesus the Parable-teller)*, Flusser wrote, "My book will have deeper effects if the reader will receive it with an open heart. It was written so that man may understand the parables of Jesus as they were intended. I would like my reader's heart to be free of the hindering rigidity of prejudices. Only in this way can Jesus' words be opened, because before the wise and the informed they are hidden. Sadly, I was forced to use much scholarship to transform my reader, to the best of my ability, into a Jewish listener to whom Jesus spoke in parables. They understood his parables; they knew what parables were, and what was expected from them. This knowledge is lost in modern man. I must make clear to my readers the essence of the rabbinical parable. Jesus' parables belonged to this essence. If pure knowledge has also gained something from this, I have no objection."[19]

Flusser's works are clear and obvious in their implication, but sad in their revelations. The barriers between the faiths remain firm because men confuse ways with goals. Bergman learned to hear the voice of the spirit wherever it spoke, and when what he heard was not clear, he listened again and again. He struggled as every great thinker does with the hidden powers that lie in words. Bergman knew that the struggle with the spirit was not simply intellectual; it was religious. Bergman grasped the power of prayer as the secret power of the soul, and we read often in the *Confessions* of Augustine, the prayers of Barock mystics like Brother Laurentius, whose prayer book he translated into Hebrew in 1950. Nothing can illustrate the genial tolerance of Bergman more than a scene which he describes in his home in 1965. Flusser had returned from India. "David attacked the Indians because of the Kali cults and the sacrifices which he had seen in Calcutta. Mosche (a friend) objected: Yet this was the way of Ramakrishna to God. David became wild. This is the superiority of the Jew, etc. I believe that Mosche is right and it is not by chance that our Monotheism had no root in India. I don't believe that there is *one* true 'way to God.' For *us* Kali would not be a way, but for the Indian our way would not be right. What is most important is the goal and not the way. We find each other in the goal. *There,* there can be no tolerance. There must, however, be a multiplicity of ways."[20]

---

[19] *Die rabbinischen Gleichnisse und der Gleichniserzaehler Jesus* (Bern, Peter Lang, 1980), 312.
[20] *Tagebuecher & Briefe*, II, 3/14/65.

Ways are many; the oneness of God is unique. This uniqueness separates God from the idols of the mind and the will. Man has come forth from nature. He is, above all its creatures, gifted with intelligence. With intelligence, he has the power to make choices. Nothing displeased Bergman more than this denigration of choice which he found in Pauline and Augustinian theology. He remained committed to these words in Deuteronomy, "Surely this instruction which I enjoin upon you this day, is not too baffling for you, nor is it beyond reach" (Deut. 30:11). He was convinced that no human condition would allow us to put aside or denigrate the efficacy of reason and its vision of the future as hope. Reason and the future remain the fundamental conditions of Jewish thought. We fear only our inabilities to comprehend and carry forth the command "to love the Lord your God, to walk in His ways, and to keep His commandments" (Deut. 30:16).

There can be no conclusion to Bergman's thought, but in a conversation he had with the theologian Jacob Taubes, many elements of Bergman's directions came together. They spoke of Hegel's relationships to Judaism. "I argued against Hegel that he was a Feuerbachian, that for him the thought of God actually confronted Abraham and Moses and commanded what he entrusted to them, never occurred. He never took seriously the Covenant as a two-sided reality. Taubes said that Hegel was a heathen like Hoelderlin, a heathen for whom the prophets' polemics, as they made themselves God from wood, would have no effect. The gods are angels which accompany men. We find it difficult to polemicize with Hegel because he stands on a finite ground. We can polemicize with Christianity, perhaps with Karl Barth, who is willing to press forward from his distant and completely other God to the God of love. The Jewish position is the fear of God. With Paul, it is completely different; it is anxiety. Paul sees God demonically with the incompleteness of the law."[21]

Bergman was a Messianic thinker and believer. He felt great sympathy with Hermann Cohen's Messianism which was the culmination of Cohen's idealism. "Time," Cohen stated, "becomes future and only future. Past and present submerge in this time of the future. This return to time is the purest idealization. All existence sinks into insignificance in the presence of the point of view of this idea, and man's existence is preserved and elevated into this being of the future. Thus, the thought of *history* comes into being for human life and for the life of the peoples.... Mankind did not live in any past and did not become alive in the present; only the future can bring about its bright and beautiful form. This is an idea, not a shadowy image of the

---

[21]*Ibid.*, 12/21/51.

beyond."[22] But it is more than idea, it is a redemption alive in a non-redeemed world, it is the presence of the sacred in the profane, the city of God in the earthly city. The future is not simply the beyond, it is the transfigured finite having become the infinite. The future lives in the present as its transfiguration, its metamorphosis. Cohen had transformed the idealism that belonged to his Kantian works through its power which he believed to be incarnated in monotheism, in the prophetic Judaism which recognized and formed the Messianism in which goodness and justice redeems the profanity of world history. Bergman's Messianism held to the same course. He struggles to affirm for Judaism what he believed was taken from her by Paul and Augustine. He fought for a reaffirmation of Messianism with its moral and intellectual idealism, its courage to accept the ideal and live in its presence. Israel was for him, the path of the prophets, a universal mission which went along with others, but preserved its uniqueness and defended its distinct universality.

The more we grasp the extent of Bergman's work and the universal quality of his endeavor, the more we become aware of the cosmic reality of his formulation of the "coincidence of opposites." These formulations are constantly being formulated, enriched and deepened in comprehension and mystery. The fundamental beginning of thinking is belief that God is life and man only its possessor. From this, Maimonidean distinction and analogy, commences a process of relationships and analogues of mediation and distinction that makes us more and more aware that the *complexio oppositorum* is the foundation in which communication links philosophy to religion and religion to philosophy. Bergman shows us the way to this communication. His life was a search for its embodiment.

---

[22]*Religion of Reason* (New York, Frederick Ungar, 1972), 249-250.

7

Faith and Parable

In 1902, Bergman in a letter to Franz Kafka, explained the differences in their perspectives upon life. Bergman and Kafka were friends. They were born in the same year, 1883, and had gone to school together. From 1893-1901, they were together in the *Altstadter Gymnasium*. In their last years, Kafka became a Socialist and Bergman a Zionist. there was considerable animosity between the two groups. Bergman noted that when the Zionists had their first public meeting in Prague in 1898, it was broken up by the Socialists and Czech assimilationists. The Jews were mainly Socialists. In 1901, both Bergman and Kafka enrolled in the University in Prague for degrees in Chemistry. Bergman finished in 1905 with mathematics, physics and philosophy, and Kafka with law. The letter of 1902 is of particular interest for the biography of Bergman. In 1972, when Bergman published his "Remembrances of Franz Kafka,"[1] there was no mention of this letter. The letter was published in the *Dairies and Letters*.

The letter begins with the question of Bergman's loyalty to Zionism. It was an issue that divided them, but it was more than an academic problem that they could easily bounce about and quickly forget. Zionism was the foundation of Bergman's life. He belonged to it spiritually and physically. It was the spiritual center of his activities. For Kafka, it was of peripheral interest. The paradoxical and parabolic qualities of life left him with a metaphysical loneliness that made it impossible for him to believe that there could be any permanent values in life. The nihilism of his attitude emerged from a fundamental conviction that there could be no relationship between man and God. Every attempt to speak of God in human language made mockery of God and revealed the blatant inadequacy of human speech.

---

[1] "Erinnerungen An Franz Kafka" in *Universitas*, July 1972.

The letter began with the question, "Why I became a Zionist? Your letter is naturally filled with mockery of my Zionism. I should cease wondering about it, and yet again and again I do wonder why you who were for a long time my school comrade don't understand my Zionism."[2] For Bergman, Zionism was his faith. This initial act is beyond explanation, but is the basis from which explanations are possible. Nothing changed very much in Bergman's life, but a depending and enhancing capacity to grasp the power of faith in himself and in others, and to comprehend its significance as the Beginning from which all values proceed. Faith laid the foundation for what would become in Bergman's thought the religious discussion. There was a separation between the friends. They had taken different paths.

Bergman complained that his belief was for Kafka only an *Idée fixe*. Kafka didn't understand that it was a part of Bergman's life that could no longer be torn out without destroying the body. "That it is a part of my body," Bergman said, "you really don't know and yet it is; it is perhaps even more. It is patched and put together from the shreds of my life. I see your laughter."[3] The lines are touching in their devotion and conviction. Bergman yearned for empathy, the profoundest of the human qualities and capacities. This empathy would become the essence of what Bergman would call the I-Thou relationship. Empathy was at its core.

"You would grasp it if you only understood yourself and me. Subconsciously," Bergman said, "you seek, since your childhood, for a content of life, and I do the same. You were brought up differently than I. You can soar to the heights of the sun and your dreams embrace the heavens. What weakens your power? You are always concerned about yourself and have the power to be alone."[4] We see Kafka emerge in a form that is very familiar to us from his writings: gifted, self-indulgent and magnificently creative. Bergman's words were prophetic. They expressed an intimacy with Kafka's character that is rare in the mountain of books that have sought to comprehend him. But this was not the issue. We are at the source of two ways of life and we realize in them the profound divisions that separate friend from friend. We witness the powers of commitment, the courage that emerges from it, but there is also a courage in skepticism and doubt. They were both dreamers. Bergman dreamed in Israel, Kafka in Prague. Bergman dreamed of Israel and Kafka of the world that was neither Israel nor Prague. He dreams in literature.

---

[2] *Tagebuecher & Briefe*, I, 1902/1903.
[3] *Ibid.*
[4] *Ibid.*

How did Bergman describe himself? "I have never dreamed much," he said, "and when I have, my dreams could not reach far because they were penetrated by raw reality.... I sought again and again...to stand alone like you but I didn't have the strength. It was my fate that I longed for others, that my heart beat warmly with love."[5] Bergman understood himself well. His need for personal relations was deep throughout his life. He needed family, friends and community. His philosophy was built on personal conversations and ties, friendship which lasted for decades, with the men of the Prague Circle, to people and thinkers from all parts of the world. Human relationship brought with it empathy, the power of reaching deeply into the being of another. In Bergman, philosophy grew from love, from its capacity to seek the Ideal and the Idea as the source and objects of love. His love emerged from love, and it was this latter love that he knew fostered every other manifestation of life.

"Don't believe," Bergman said, "that it was compassion which made me a Zionist. My Zion is proper egoism. I feel that I would like to fly, to create and cannot. I no longer have the power. I feel that in other relationships, I have the strength, that the unborn capacity has in no way left me, I only do not have the strength."[6] It is difficult to approach Bergman's feelings and his expressions of lack of strength, but there is great clarity in his faith in Zion. We have the feeling that he had made an irreversible decision and although it came at an early age, it revealed a way that he would travel until his death. Bergman never claimed to be a Kafka specialist and there is no reason to believe that he read everything Kafka wrote. He knew him as a friend in days when Jewish life in Prague produced great intellectual figures, made substantial contributions to German literature, and aroused the opposition of the Czech majority. The possibility of a symbiosis was vague and uncertain. Jewish energy rushed forward in a new direction; the dream of the Land of Israel. This direction awaited the visions of the poetic and the intellectual, the words of Martin Buber and the imaginative powers of other great personalities. Bergman knew what this all meant, and the heroic powers it demanded. It is not strange that he felt weak when he glimpsed the enormity of the task, the going forth to the new land.

Bergman explained that "Zionism is for me the expression for my longing for love. Since I am aware that thousands of others will suffer like me, I will go and work with them. Could I at least empathize with them?"[7] The words bear the mark of a young romantic who longs for the

---
[5] *Ibid.*
[6] *Ibid.*
[7] *Ibid.*

strength to bear the burdens of his dreams, who needs to discover others to share the responsibilities, but who is convinced that the cause is urgent and just and the sacrifice is commanded. Here we witness the love that Zion kindled in Bergman, and Buber was to enflame. Buber's *Speeches on Judaism* would be the light that would create the community and the destiny that Zionists would share with each other.

Bergman continued, "Perhaps we will yet overcome the weakness, stand strong on our own soil, and not be like a reed swinging in the wind as if uprooted, perhaps, I will find once again my strength. Often it seems to me that I can fly but then my power is broken and my wings become lame. I would like for once to stand on our own soil and not feel rootless. Perhaps then my powers will return."[8] With these words, the letter ends and we realize that the childhood friendship of Kafka and Bergman had radically changed. The young men were forced into different paths and would live different lives.

Eighteen years later, in 1920, Bergman went to Palestine and became a distinguished philosopher. Kafka became a writer admired throughout the world. Bergman's Zionism was present in his family. In Kafka's it was absent. "The father, Siegmund Bergman," Hans Tramer stated, "had been one of the founders of the *Volksverein*, and Johanna, his mother, was one of the driving forces in the women's Zionist group."[9] In his "Remembrances," Bergman spoke of the atheistic and pantheistic atmosphere in which Kafka lived. He mentioned that "Kafka sought with all means to take my faith from me, and plagued me with constant discussions. I had justified anxieties about losing my faith, and the beauty of the Passover season which I loved so much. I hoped to hold on at least until Passover. I succeeded. This time Franz did not conquer me."[10]

These discussions were the directional signs that indicated the roads that each friend would follow. They go beyond themselves toward distinct world views. There is a point when the distance between the roads became so great that a new qualitative relationship took place. We can imagine that the atheism, the paradoxes and the sense of despair in Kafka's works offered him little. To the believer this literature of despair and resignation only revealed a world from which God had withdrawn. Bergman lived with the presence of God and acted in response to it. He could not live in Kafka's world.

---

[8]*Ibid.*
[9]"Prague – City of Three Peoples" in *Leo Baeck Institute Year Book* IX (London, East and West Library, 1964), 316.
[10]"Erinnerungen An Franz Kafka," 742.

If it seemed that Bergman struggled with his faith, which is a usual experience among all great believers, we are sure that he was not willing to surrender it. In 1912, the philosopher Franz Brentano had written to Carl Stumpf in Berlin on behalf of Bergman. The problem was the possibility of an academic position; but the real problem concerned the possibility of Bergman's conversion. In reply to Brentano's letter describing Stumpf's unfriendliness, Bergman spoke of his refusal to consider conversion. He stated, "I know many converted Jews. I have such in mine and my wife's family. I always observed that those who made such a step without true conviction justified themselves to themselves and to others by saying that they observed in themselves a laughable skepticism toward religion. Neither one nor another religion has value, and consequently, a religious change is meaningless. The truth is that one or another religion is a worthy institution only if it is inwardly experienced. Only such an inwardness is basic for the Ideal of a unity of religion."[11]

Bergman gave up the idea of an academic position in Berlin and his correspondence with Carl Stumpf showed clearly the way that led to Jerusalem and not to Berlin. Faith received the command to leave the land for a new land, to search for the freedom to find an air that could be breathed. Prague was now only a preparation for the journey. "Away from here," were Kafka's words, but what they meant to Bergman was Palestine and Zionism.

In the conclusion to his remembrances of his early years of friendship with Kafka, was a question which the editor of *Universitas* put to him, "To what extent can we speak of a turn toward the religious world, toward the tradition of the Jewish faith in Kafka's last years?" Bergman again stressed the fact that he was not a scholar of Kafka's writings but only a friend. He said, however, that he would like to comment on one of Kafka's last stories, "The Investigations of a Dog." Bergman then remarked, "I would like at first to stress how correct is the form of the question. The religious world is not simply identifiable with the tradition of the Jewish faith although Kafka often identified them. He sought to escape isolation and find union with the sources (*Mutterboden*), the tradition which was not given to him in his father's house. The experience of the Yiddish theatre troop in the shabby cafe symbolized the depths of his longing. This latter feeling is unique and very well revealed in 'The Investigations of a Dog.'"[12]

Bergman accepted the idea that Kafka inclined toward a religious world and was deeply concerned about his Jewish origins. Bergman was

---

[11]*Tagebuecher*, 1/5/12.
[12]"Erinnerungen," 749.

sure that whenever a man became a serious thinker, there was a concern for the religious question. The depths of thought and morality were too closely knit to the truths of religious faith to exist without a relationship to them. Although he never considered Kafka a religious thinker, he knew that Kafka never simply freed himself of his religious concerns. The more profoundly we penetrate the core of man's spiritual life, the more we are aware of how intimately it is tied to faith, tradition, hope and love.

A year before his death, Bergman recalled the words that Kafka wrote in an album he had received as a present when he was thirteen years old. He wrote, "There is a coming and a going, a separation – and often no return." Bergman spoke of the specific task of the Jews to bridge the differences between peoples. "We grew up in Prague," he said, "a city in which three peoples lived, the Czechs, the Germans and the Jews; they lived *together* in spite of oppositions. The greatest achievement of the Bohemian Jews was that they built *bridges*. The works of Kafka and Max Brod are living witnesses of this achievement which was this *Brueckendasein*. Kafka felt it and stated it in his famous *Letter to His Father* that the Jew must first be a Jew to fulfill this synthetic function within mankind. Max Brod and Felix Weltsch could do what they did for the Czech people and for the German only from such a synthetic universal view."[13]

Bergman approached Kafka with the hope of seeing in his writings his own understanding of history, of Prague and Jews of the Prague Circle. Bergman gave a unique voice to what Brod called the *Prague Circle*, which he believed had a distinct and unique role to play in the formation of a philosophy for the Jews and the future of Israel. There was always the universalism and the synthesis of traditions. The enemy was nationalism in its vulgar racial formulations which turned people against people. Bergman changed little from the time of his letter to Kafka to his formulation of a cosmic philosophy of religion.

It was in "The Investigations of a Dog" that Bergman found the religious word that he sought in Kafka. The reflections that came with these investigations led the reader in many directions, but no reader comes to an author without a point of view and struggles to realize or oppose it in his own reality. Speaking of history, the narrator, the dog investigator, noted that "our generation is lost, it may be, but it is more blameless than those earlier ones." Why is this the natural response? We are told that conditions have changed. Previously, the edifice of dogdom was still loosely put together, the true Word could still have intervened, planning or replanning the structure, changing it at will, transforming it

---

[13]*Tagebuecher*, 1/22/74.

Faith and Parable

into its opposite, and the Word was there, was very near at least on the tip of everybody's tongue, anyone might have hit upon it."[14] We immediately make analogies to our own comprehension of the revealed Word and we ask whether it has been lost in a similar way. Kafka was always aware that there was a gulf between the Message and its realization, and he wondered if it ever became a living reality or remained a phantom here and there, visible and then invisible for the man who searches for it but in fact, only dreams of it.

We assume that spiritual change precedes physical change. We observe changes in history and we realize "that change begins in the soul before it appears in ordinary existence, and that when they began to enjoy a dog's life, they must already have possessed a real old dog's soul and were by no means so near their starting point as they thought, or as their eyes feasting on all doggish joys tried to persuade them." No matter what we think about our history, there are so many diverse opinions that it is hard to believe that we belong to the same race. "Why not believe that all dogs from the beginning of time have been my colleagues, all diligent in their own way, all unsuccessful in their own way, all silent or falsely garrulous in their own way, as hapless research is apt to make one?"[15]

We approach a problem that had been very significant for Bergman: the need for a new conception of mankind, a change in man's moral nature, the reality of a new Ideal that brings with it the realization how little science depends upon a movement that originates in God and flows toward man. The only science we now know is a causal-mechanistic one. "Our scientific knowledge," the investigator tells us, "which generally makes for an extreme specialization is remarkably simple in one province where it teaches that the earth engenders our food, and then, after having laid down this hypothesis, gives the method by which the different foods may be achieved in their best kinds and greatest abundance."[16]

But the matter is not that simple, the movement of food is not from below, our science has not yet discovered other dimensions of knowledge, those which emerge from divine outflow. Our investigator believed that "the main part of the food that is discovered on the ground in such cases, comes from above – in saying that, however, I am saying nothing against science; the earth of course, brings forth this kind of food too.... Whether the earth draws one kind of food out of itself and calls

---

[14]"Investigations of a Dog" in *Franz Kafka: The Complete Stories* (New York, Schocken Books, 1972), 300.
[15]*Ibid.*, 300, 301-302.
[16]*Ibid.*, 302-303.

down another kind from the skies, perhaps makes no essential difference, and science, which has established that in both cases it is necessary to prepare the ground, need not perhaps concern itself with such distinctions...."[17] Kafka hints that science does take a "veiled interest" in such matters but this would be a new science, it would say much more than what is now being said, "If you have food in your jaws you have solved all questions for the time being." From the question of movement and limitation, Bergman believed that Kafka grasped the problem that was the constant concern of his thinking. The friends had found the beginnings of their reconciliation.

Science recognized more than the preparation of the ground; it sought a "perfecting process of incantation, dance and song." The productivity of food demands the work of the total human being. There is the power of prayer and Bergman never doubted its efficacy. The work of science includes prayer. The spiritual powers of man include not only the intellect, but the emotive powers. These work together with thinking, and belong to it intimately. Man is a being who for purposes of analysis can be separated into different categories of activities, but whatever the divisions, they remain equally parts of the same being, the thinking, acting, judging being. Bergman, who believed that science was an expression of the fullness of being, refused to allow that fullness to be defined as only analytical and dialectical reason. These were permeated by man's longing for realities above and beyond reason; they were strengthened and enhanced by the concentrative force of prayer.

The investigator knew that "the scratching and watering of the ground...served to produce both kinds of food and remains indispensable; incantation, dance, and song, however, are concerned less with the ground food in the narrower sense and serve principally to attract the food from above. Tradition fortifies one in this interpretation. The ordinary dogs themselves set science right here without knowing it, and without science being able to venture a reply."[18] Bergman was deeply impressed by these descriptions. He believed that science was more than the fixed dimensions of causality. He knew that Kafka had touched the fundamental truth of reality when he caused the investigator to remark that it was a remarkable thing "the people in all their ceremonies gaze upwards." "I simply cannot conceive," the investigator said, "how the learned can bear to let our people, unruly and passionate as they are, chant their incantations with their faces turned upwards, wail our ancient folk songs into the air, and spring high in their dances as

---

[17]*Ibid.*, 303.
[18]*Ibid.*, 303-304.

Faith and Parable

though, forgetting the ground, they wished to take flight from it forever."[19]

What was only an experiment would finally become a truth. There were many sorts of proof and if the experiment did not suit all scientists, it did bring forth its own truth in faith. The investigator stated that he "did not believe the scientist's depreciation of my experiment, yet belief was of no avail here, but only proof, and I resolved to set about establishing that and thus raise my experiment from its original irrelevance and set it in the very center of the field of research. I wished to prove that when I retreated before the food, it was not the ground that attracted it at a slant but I who drew it after me."[20] The problem that we confront in new ways of thinking is not with science but with our fellow men. Science has enough "elasticity to admit exceptions and isolated cases" but what would the "other dogs say?"

Bergman felt confirmed in his view that Kafka had returned in some way to the traditions of his people. He believed that Kafka's references to the Fathers (Urvaeter) indicated a deep respect for the sources of tradition. The investigator stated that "our forefathers appeared threateningly before me." The experiments had tired him but they were there before him and "I bow before their knowledge, it came from sources of which we know no longer, and for that reason, much as I may feel compelled to oppose them, I shall never overstep their laws, but content myself with wriggling out through the gaps for which I have a particularly good nose."[21]

There emerges from these struggles a new concept of science, a new knowledge and a broader imagination that envisions a reality which is not only progressive, horizontal and secularly historical, but vertical, making us realize that man has the power to draw down from the heavens forces that change and reform his reality. The heavens are not empty, and reality has not been handed over exclusively to human reason. Man looks upwards and his food comes forth from divine incarnation, as well as from his physical and rational efforts. No longer can they be separated, no longer can one be profane and the other sacred; they are all sacred as they are called forth from man's incantations. His physical efforts and his prayers work together. They reveal powers which in separation no longer exist.

The investigator could say with clarity and confidence that "it was this instinct (knowing the powers of incantation) that made one – and perhaps for the sake of science itself, but a different science from that of

---

[19] *Ibid.*, 304.
[20] *Ibid.*, 306.
[21] *Ibid.*, 309-310.

today, an ultimate science – prize freedom higher than everything else. Freedom! Certainly such freedom as is possible today is a wretched business. But nevertheless freedom, nevertheless a possession."[22] Bergman cited these final words of the story because they could have equally been his. Bergman read Kafka from the perspective of his friendship, from his knowledge of Prague and from his recollections of truths and beliefs that confirmed his assumption that the Jews had a distinct role to play in history, a role they played in Prague, and a role they would exercise in Jerusalem. Bergman believed that the sources must never be lost and although the interpretations change, there is a constancy of faith and devotion. In the sources lived the people and the community. He was sure in the end that Kafka knew this. He didn't know how deep was Kafka's faith, but there was recognition and devotion.

Bergman's interpretation is viable. We know that every great literary achievement defies "orthodox" interpretations. Bergman was a friend of many years, a friend of Kafka's friends, a lover of the same city, of the university, the clubs, the homes where they gathered for social evenings, the home of Bertha Fanta, Bergman's mother-in-law, one of the centers of Prague's social and intellectual life. Kafka, Bergman believed, emerged from his early socialism to religious Zionism, close to the faith of Bergman.

If we look back on Kafka's work, if we think about the philosophy of Bergman, we realize how differently both men journeyed in their lives. Bergman began in faith and ended in it; Kafka in the aesthetics of literature, in paradox and parable. In the end, it all seemed to be parable even if the vision changed and the content approached tradition, faith, and ritual. From faith to faith we were led to a cosmic philosophy; it was joined by Sri Aurobindo, Rav Kook, Teilhard de Chardin; it embodied East and West, philosophy and theosophy, pantheism and Yoga, its embrace was astonishing and demanded heroic imaginative powers and beliefs. There was a place for parables and paradoxes, but only a limited place. The latter had to be overcome and surpassed. Bergman could not stop with Kafka; he had worlds to embrace and cried out only for the strength to read and to write. In the latter he found prayer.

Bergman sought throughout his life to give reality to his faith in God. He sought the way of the philosopher, the lover of wisdom, the man who not only looked ahead, but who found in his heavenly glance the sources of new powers and courage. He was an artist, as well as a thinker. He brought together the truths that embraced both. As the artist, he was the inventor; he knew that reality could not be created logically, that it was

---

[22]*Ibid.*, 316.

Faith and Parable

the work of the hands, the ears and the taste, it was the consequence of man's forging powers of invention and form. The philosopher was always the artist, the formulator of the words that forged the realization of ideas, that allowed them to speak morally and politically, that caused them to influence the thoughts and actions of other men.

Bergman didn't build a single structure, he constructed many forms, many dialogues; he created visions. His work showed his ways; they were signs and symbols that each man could follow or put aside. Each was a meaningful and attractive configuration; each had a hint of the beautiful, and only awaited its form. He endowed his works with the love that flowed from him to his creations, and from his creations back to himself. He was the philosopher in whom others could love philosophy. He never took away their problems, he encouraged their freedom to form attitudes and views. He, like others, knew what it meant to love not only the works we bring forth, but the sources that make these works possible: the indwelling divine spirit.

8

Friendship of Great Men

From 1910 to 1912, Albert Einstein was professor of physics in Prague. During these years, a friendship developed between him and Hugo Bergman which was to continue until Einstein's death in 1955. Their friendship brought together two men whose interests in the future of mankind, in man's critical judgment, and in the powers of his imagination, made it possible for them to communicate and trust each other. They were Europeans in the most distinctive and distinguished sense; their vision was universal. They shared a love of the cosmos. They admired creative work, and were deeply devoted to the survival of Israel. Einstein came to a provincial city famous for its intellectual life. Bergman has given us an account of the friendship, and it is from it that we construct a picture of men who lived with ideas and struggled for their realization. Bergman described Prague at the time, as "a tri-national town, inhabited by a Czech majority and the German and Jewish minorities. These minorities, however, were the intellectual leaders. The German University was of international renown. I need only mention the name of Ernst Mach, who for four years occupied the chair of physics. And Prague's poets who wrote in German – Rilke, Kafka, Werfel – have conquered the world. The German Theatre, under the Jew Angel Neumann, played a leading role in the German cultural life of the time."[1] In this city, Bergman and Einstein became friends.

Bergman attended Einstein's Seminar. He had already acquired his doctorate and belonged to a philosophical circle of disciples of the philosopher Anton Marty, whose interest was the philosophy of language. The group was called the "Louvre Circle," after the coffeehouse in which it met. "Later on," Bergman remarked, "we got

---

[1] "Personal Remembrances of Albert Einstein" in *Boston Studies in the Philosophy of Science*, Vol. XIII (Dordrecht, D. Reidel Publishing Co.), 388.

together in the drawing room of my then mother-in-law, Berta Sohr-Fanta, where Einstein was a frequent visitor when we were reading Hegel's *Phenomenology of the Spirit*. I scarcely remember whether Einstein took part in these readings. Yet I recall well the very popular lecture he held before this score of nonphysicists on the special theory of relativity."[2] Bergman recalled that he accompanied Einstein to his home after seminar, and that it was in Fanta's salon that Einstein met the pianist Ottilie Nagel, with whom he played duets, he the violin, she the piano.

Bergman remembered a particular conversation that concerned Einstein's work, his search for cosmic equations. "Actually," he said, "I am glad to be allowed to lecture on these elementary matters, for in my own research, it often happens that I pursue and explore some thoughts, only to realize in the end that I have been wandering in a maze; all those weeks of hunting a phantom would have been lost, had I not been giving my lectures and thus doing something useful during all that time."[3] These speculative wanderings were deeply appreciated by Bergman. They had also become an integral part of his own life and he knew that without them reason grew restrictive and dogmatic. Bergman had become acquainted with the theosophist, Rudolf Steiner, whose works remained a constant influence throughout his life. Bergman remembered the Steiner lectures in Prague. One evening, he told Einstein that he would attend the Steiner lecture and Einstein prepared to accompany him. Einstein and Steiner had little in common at this moment. In 1953, when Bergman visited Einstein at Princeton, he noticed that the latter was immersed in a book on parapsychology that had just been published and Einstein "said to me – as if interested and repelled at the same time – 'It (the book) can't be true.'"[4]

Bergman stated that during the two years of his acquaintance with Einstein in Prague, he didn't remember any discussion about Judaism or Jews. All civil servants in the Hapsburg Empire had to state religious preference. Einstein joined the Jewish group; but this was a mere formality. "It was only ten years later," Bergman remarked, "that Einstein, under the influence of the German Zionist leader Kurt Blumenfeld, came closer to Judaism and in particular to Zionism, whose faithful servant he was to become later."[5]

In 1919, Bergman was in London when the London press heralded the "Scientific Revolution! Newton's Theory confuted by the research of

---

[2] *Ibid.*, 399.
[3] *Ibid.*, 390.
[4] *Ibid.*
[5] *Ibid.*, 390-391.

a German Physicist!" Einstein had become world famous. "I had become sort of a newspaper celebrity," he said to Bergman in 1953. The war had just ended, there was no peace treaty between Germany and Great Britain, and the English celebrated the victory of a German scientist over Newton. Bergman was impressed by this recognition of greatness that went beyond the walls of national pride. A year later, Bergman emigrated to Palestine. There, he would foster a philosophical universalism that sought peace with the Arabs and often isolated him and his friends, the Brit Shalom group, from the political realism of those who found little reality in philosophy.

The first visit of Einstein to Jerusalem was in 1923. Einstein was returning from lectures in Japan to Berlin. Bergman remarked on Einstein's impression of Japan. He noted his statement "that the Japanese employed human beings where we would use machines." Bergman took cognizance of this remark because it reflected Einstein's social interest and "concern for the fate of the working man."[6] In Tel Aviv, Einstein addressed a group of workers who received him warmly. Their organization was the *Histadrut*, the national labor force in Palestine and Israel.

His speech on Mount Scopus, above the Mount of Olives, was the great event in Jerusalem. The University was beginning to take form. Its first building had been purchased and the future university established. Menachem Ussishkin was in charge of activities. The event was monumental. Ussishkin asked Einstein to step forward and said, "Mount the rostrum that has been waiting for you these past 2000 years." Bergman's description continues, "With a slightly ironical smile Einstein played his role in this theatrical performance and, after Ussishkin's bombastic words, began to lecture on the theory of relativity in his simple, unadorned German. This was the first lecture of The Hebrew University held two years before its inauguration."[7] We imagine the event today with a sublime and fateful feeling. Both the human person and the universe of reason had begun its life in this ancient city, on a sacred place. The construction of a university was begun where men and women of all faiths would come to study and learn together for the betterment of mankind. Bergman, whose life symbolized this event, would himself become a figure of peace and humaneness. His professorship embodied a universality of extraordinary intensity and a sublime openness to man's search for divinity.

In 1929, Einstein attempted to speak to the problem of the Jewish-Arab conflict. After the first Arab riots, Einstein was asked by the editor,

---
[6]*Ibid.*, 391.
[7]*Ibid.*, 392.

Achmed Achtar, to suggest a solution to the problem. Achtar was the editor of a newly founded English language weekly. On February 25, 1930, Einstein wrote, "Our (the Jews and Arabs) position is bad because Jews and Arabs are opposing each other as warring parties in the face of a third factor – the British Mandatory power. Such a position is beneath the dignity of both peoples, and it can only be improved through an understanding between ourselves." He proposed a council of Jews and Arabs in equal numbers. "The discussions of this council should be secret and resolutions could be published in the name of the whole council only if they were carried by at least three votes (each group had four votes) on each side."[8] Achtar accepted the plan and felt honored that it had been proposed by Einstein.

Where do we find men who would be beyond the nationalism that fixed their peoples? The philosopher's voice gives authenticity to the situation, but the latter has a life of its own and follows the course of actions which are dictated to it, forces over which there is little control. Men like Martin Buber and Bergman would again and again attempt to interfere in political life. Their words would be praised and stored away for future historians. They had little immediate impact. They nevertheless continued to speak. The situation of one day does not necessarily become the fate of the next. Man in situations has immediate responsibilities which must be exercised; man is judged by what he does and how he does it. Man is also beyond situation and he speaks of the future; he speaks of hope. He speaks for those of his fellow men and they judge him for what he says.

In Bergman's *Diaries* there is a letter to Einstein. Bergman thanked him for a copy of the volume which the Library of Living Philosophers dedicated to Einstein on his seventieth birthday. Bergman told him that his "first view fell upon his explanations of physics as the 'attempt to grasp being as something conceptual, what is thought as independent of empirical becoming.' It is very beautiful how you emphasize twice in this formulation the conceptual-constructive character of physics, contrary to every naive realism which separates the physical event from human thinking, and would like to establish the former for itself, causing, from the beginning, an obstacle."[9]

Bergman had always been interested in the philosophy of science and in 1928 published a study of causality from Kant to Anton Marty, Bolzano, Brentano, N. Hartmann. Einstein, who was at the time in Berlin, wrote in his "Foreword": "It is well known that present-day physics, influenced by the facts of atomic physics, places in serious doubt

---

[8]*Ibid.*, 392-393.
[9]*Tagebuecher & Briefe*, 3/6/50.

Friendship of Great Men 111

the feasibility of a rigorous causality. This difficulty will probably be rectified when a philosophy specialist, praiseworthy for the unusual extent of his knowledge of philosophical literature, his independence of thought, and his knowledge of the actual relevant physical facts, along with attempted explanations of those facts, analyzes the problem. May this little book contribute to promoting the best in our present-day attempts at merging physical and philosophical thought."[10]

In the same letter, Bergman urged Einstein to come again to Israel to speak about education and teaching. Bergman was deeply disturbed by the inordinate concern for military preparedness in Israel. The future is endangered if we make of the military a virtue, if the needs of the moment become the absorbing passion of the people. We need a future vision and this he believed Einstein could offer. Bergman believed that great human beings could influence the people and that their words would be acted upon. This was a belief he refused to surrender to the cynical and skeptical realists around him. He, like Buber, knew despair of isolation in their own land. They would work with faith and hope; this was their fate. This faith was the source of Bergman's life. It was the foundation of his work. He knew that there were two strengths which the philosopher needed to pursue his work: faith and prayer. Neither one could be explained, because they went beyond explanation and could only be its source. Every strength, faithfulness, and certainty emerged from faith and prayer. The latter were risks which only the believer could pursue. What else could man ask of God but the strength to continue his work and to do it with greater conviction and desire. The believer was plagued with the street cleverness of those who assumed that they alone understood the foe-friendship conflict of power struggles. The believer knew, in addition, there were rights and wrongs, the latter however, required patience, persistence and endurance. For that we pray; our strength needs the strength that comes from above.

In 1953, Bergman traveled to the United States. He spent time with Einstein at Princeton. "Our conversation," Bergman stated, "lasted one and a half hours and dealt almost exclusively with actual problems of physics. Einstein explained to me the tragic tension between himself and the younger generation of physicists: his pupils had adopted the statistical method that had developed in physics as a consequence of the quantum theory, whereas he himself refused to go along with them and to admit that God casts the die. Although he had revolutionized physics, his own thinking was too deeply influenced by classical conceptions for

---

[10]*The Controversy Concerning the Law of Causality* in *Contemporary Physics* (Dordrecht, D. Reidel Publishing Co.) 395.

him to be prepared to acknowledge that *chance* had a place in physics."[11] He spoke to Bergman of the "World Formula," but told him that there was no way to prove it. "Thus my World Formula," he said, "is like a locked box that cannot be opened." He laughed while telling me of a search that cost him many years of his life.

Bergman noted that the "world admired, even adored Einstein, whilst he saw himself and his work objectively as part of the universe. "My internal and external life," he once said, "depend so much on the work of *others* that I must make an extreme effort to give as much as I have received."[12] Bergman ended his account feeling that there was a fundamental religious source to Einstein's thought. It lay in his feeling of belonging to the universe, a thinker whose work made a difference in human thought. This work was already prepared in the thought of others. Einstein was a man of the universe, prepared by it to bring forth those "leaps" which change radically the course of mankind.

Einstein, as we mentioned, wrote a "Foreword" to Bergman's book on causality; it revealed the importance of a philosophical approach to a scientific problem. The thinker must always be aware of the process of his thinking, its limitation and the possibilities of surpassing them. In his conclusion to that book, Bergman stated, "The presupposition of determinism – may it now be the rigorous law of causality, or may it be the looser law of probability – has lucidly shown itself to be a requirement we attribute to the world construed by us from physical appearances for the purpose of its construction. We certainly do not want to undervalue this construction and abstraction, but while we recognize the limits of them as the work of men and do not confuse the artful reality of physics with the immediately experienced reality, this reality discloses to us its true significance, the universally true significance of science and culture: to raise the intellect to consciousness of itself in its own works."[13]

This awareness of the freedom of the intellect is nothing other than the free act of the will. We are aware of this freedom in the power to think of the laws of causality as tools of the intellect, as hypothesis with which we are capable of constructing and forming a science for the universe. The tools of our construction are the conjectures by which we give a spiritual order to the world about us, relate references to each other, knowing at the same time that what we are doing refers to the capacity of our tools. Bergman did not remain with the problem of physics. His concerns embraced man's moral and religious future. In

---

[11]*Personal Remembrances*, 393.
[12]*Ibid*.
[13]*Controversy Concerning the Law of Causality*, 461.

Friendship of Great Men 113

1971, Bergman wrote to his lifelong friend Robert Weltsch about a small book that he was then reading. The book was written by the philosopher Georg Picht (1913-1982), and called *Mut zur Utopie* (1966) (Courage for Utopia). In the letter, Bergman stated, "I am more and more convinced that only a *moral* new direction will make a solution to all difficulties possible, however utopian it is. Do you know the book of Georg Picht? He shows that the whole difficulty of your position stems from technology. In the next decade – he speaks of years – there must be a catastrophe for mankind if there is not a radical change in mankind's consciousness."[14] Bergman remained constantly open to such ideas. He saw their visions, and set aside the inadequacies of their detail. He felt, like Einstein, that he was a man of the universe, deeply dependent upon it, and owing it his life. Here lay the powers of his religious faith; here he believed lay Einstein's religiosity.

Einstein and Bergman were friends, although after 1912 they saw each other rarely. Their friendship lay in their openness to visions, their concern for the meaning of Israel, and their devotion to the universality of reason as freedom. They were artists of the intellect. We view their friendship with admiration and respect. It reflects the respect that emerges in us for the inner moral sentiment, and the heavenly order above us, but even more the evolution that draws us from one to the other, from the higher to the lower, and from the lower to the higher.

Einstein spoke of the "World Formula," Bergman of a "jump" in evolution "comparable to the 'jump' which creates a new species in the plant or animal kingdom." Alongside their visions, another came along, to strengthen our faith in man's rational powers, a figure whose thought has caused fear for many and excitement for others. This figure was Pierre Teilhard de Chardin (1881-1955), who told us that under "the combined pressure of science and philosophy, we are being forced, experientially and intellectually, to accept the world as a coordinated system of activity which is gradually rising up toward freedom and consciousness. The only satisfactory way of interpreting this process is to regard it as irreversible and convergent. Thus, ahead of us, a *universal cosmic center* is taking on definition, in which everything reaches its term, in which everything is explained, is felt and is ordered."[15] This Jesuit Father found his way easily into Bergman's world. Like all those with whom he found communion and spiritual friendship, Teilhard de Chardin spoke of cosmic reality in which the development of mankind found a central place as it moved toward its divine end that gave it movement and purpose.

---

[14]*Tagebuecher*, 11/2/71.
[15]*How I Believe* (New York, Harper & Row, 1969), 79-80.

The friendship of great men belongs to their souls. Their souls communicate with each other through the destinies they have acquired, and the work they must carry forth. Their communion is their fate. They have learned their freedom in their dependence upon others, but, above all, their dependence upon the universe is the consciousness of the universe's dependence on them. They have cosmic citizenship which alone is capable of satisfying their need for universality and unity.

9

From Theory to Practice

This chapter originated with a footnote to a sermon delivered by Albert Schweitzer. The note described a short and beautifully written text of Hugo Bergman on a blessing, *Der Segenspruch*. The text was introduced by a comparison between Bergman and the Greek figure Nestor, the wise adviser to the heroes of the age. Bergman was named the "Nestor of the Jewish philosophers."[1]

What is of importance is the closeness between Schweitzer's concept of *"die Ehrfurcht vor dem Leben,"* (the reverence for life), and Bergman's small but precious work on the blessing. At times we find that the most valuable texts of a philosopher are short and unique pieces. This is certainly true of Bergman's work. In his diary for July 20, 1943, Bergman remarked that he copied some sublime words on love from Schweitzer. He noted these words: "Dear God, should I write a letter rather than say my evening prayer? How shall I find my way in life? I seek a way to You, to the One whom I need. For me it is like cutting through a jungle of obligations through which I seem unable to penetrate and create a path. Letters which I must write, books which I will read, and the necessary inquiries that the many endure and constantly put aside, are as if I removed one barrier, resolved one obligation, and ten take their place. I cannot be rid of them. How then can I find my way to You?"[2]

Bergman's continuous search was "to seek a way to You." When he wrote of his remembrances of his childhood friend, Franz Kafka, he spoke in particular of his story "Investigations of a Dog," where the problem of sources arose. From what source do we derive our food, caused innumerable investigations. This looming and disquieting

---

[1] Albert Schweitzer, *Was Sollen Wir Tun?* Ed. Martin Strege and Lothar Stiehm (Heidelberg, Lambert Schneider, 1974). Notes to Sermon 3 by Lothar Stiehm.
[2] Hugo Bergman, *Tagebuecher und Briefe*, 7/20/43.

question always created opposition. One thesis enunciated this proposition: "If you have food in your jaws, you have solved all questions for the time being." There was, however, the contrary thesis: "The main parts of the food that are discovered on the ground in such cases come from above."[3]

Science teaches the people to remain bound to the soil, to see in it the source of nourishment, but now comes "this remarkable thing; the people in all their ceremonies gaze upwards."[4] Kafka showed that after all the experimentation and investigation, it was not the ground that drew the food from above "but I who drew it after me.... Although in reality I was laboring to annul the findings of science, I felt within me a deep reassurance, indeed almost the proverbial serenity of the scientific worker. In my thought, I begged forgiveness of science; there must be room for my researches too."[5]

Where has Bergman taken us with these remarks on Kafka, with the quotations from Schweitzer, if not to the realization that man must seek beyond the self to discover the truth of his reality and that of the world? He must seek a space where the impossible become possible. The nourishment that comes from above makes it possible for us to understand that which comes from the earth. Their relationship is intimate and necessary. Their reality depends upon each other. In the absolutes of science, man is blinded to the world above him. In the exclusivity of the vision above, man loses the efficacy of his reason and his responsibility to creation. He loses that incontrovertible wisdom that links heaven and earth in responsibility and dependence.

What, we should ask, ties Bergman to Schweitzer and in particular to these sermons which he gave after World War I, and to his philosopher of culture? It was Ernst Cassirer who pointed to the unique message of Schweitzer in a world becoming destructively mad with nationalism and dictatorships. Cassirer, in his inaugural lecture at the University of Goteborg, Sweden, in 1935, spoke of Schweitzer's message, of his *conceptus cosmicus*, of his universal concept of philosophy which Kant enunciated in "The Architectonic of Pure Reason" at the end of his *Critique of Pure Reason*. Cassirer quoted these words from Schweitzer's lectures delivered earlier at Uppsala in 1922: "Now it is evident for all that the self-annihilation of culture is in process. Also, what remains of it is no longer certain.... Every effort should have been made to direct the attention of the educated and the uneducated to the problem of cultural ideals.... But in the hour of peril, the watchman slept, who should have

---

[3] Franz Kafka, *The Complete Stories*, 303.
[4] *Ibid.*, 304.
[5] *Ibid.*, 306-308.

From Theory to Practice 117

kept watch over us. So it happened that we did not struggle for our culture."[6]

Often repeated, we hear again and again these words: "The watchman slept." We try to give ourselves a vision and an ideal of philosophy. We ask about our desires to make philosophy scientific, to be immersed in analyses and description. We know that we have a penchant for definition and taxology. Are we being philosophers in all this science? Schweitzer showed another way, deeply appreciated by Cassirer and followed in many ways by Bergman.

Philosophers have been derided as dreamers to be left alone with their ideas and ideals. The lives of the philosophers give lie to these accusations. We need not relate the lines of Schweitzer, of Cassirer and of Bergman. Their lives are commitments to ideas; their words expressions of danger, and the courage that they brought to them. Again in 1944, a year before his death, Cassirer, in a lecture at Connecticut College, urged his audience to study Schweitzer's Uppsala lectures. "If you study these lectures," he said, "you will be amazed to find here a perfect diagnosis of the present crisis of human culture."[7]

Equally penetrating and decisive was the impression Schweitzer made on Toni Cassirer in 1934 at Oxford. "What he said," she remarked, "seemed so startlingly simple that I could hardly trust my ears. He spoke of the decline of our civilization, and based it upon such simple motives that I, happily and astonished, found my own thoughts in them, which I dared to express to Ernst because from me, they were rejected as not being 'modern.'" Schweitzer had no such problem. The secret of his power of conviction lay fundamentally in this "not modern simplification of basic principles."[8]

Suddenly, we find ourselves confronted by a philosopher whose life-philosophy found a place to develop, and from which it could communicate in easily understood terms the moral obligations of man, the need to alleviate pain, to comprehend the reverence for life, to address our fellow men, and our children, showing them a way that gives to each his or her right to education and moral development. Schweitzer incorporated his Uppsala lectures in his easily readable book, *The Philosophy of Civilization*. He enumerated the responsibilities that each of us must take for family, society, and mankind. "In the hour of peril," he observed, "the watchman who ought to have kept us awake

---

[6]*Symbol, Myth, and Culture*. Essays and Lectures of Ernst Cassirer, 1935-1945. (New Haven: Yale University Press, 1979), 60.
[7]"Philosophy and Politics" in *Symbol, Myth, and Culture,* 231.
[8]Toni Cassirer, *Mein Leben mit Ernst Cassirer* (Hildesheim, Gerstenberg Verlag, 1981), 236-237.

was himself asleep, and the result was that we put up no fight at all on behalf of our civilization."[9] Schweitzer showed how futile was our Scholastic philosophy when the world needed the clear and decisive voice of the watchman.

The philosopher bears in him a vocation to be the guardian of reason, to be the courageous combatant for the ideals of a civilization, to have the commitment to freedom, and to make the wager in the faith of our reason, to proclaim the right to philosophical faith. Schweitzer began his 1919 sermon with a statement about the fundamental law of ethics. He said: "We see in the previous sermons that the basic ethical law is reverence before life, a sympathy for and an experiencing of what the living being around us suffers."[10]

The opening biblical verse stated that, "righteous man knows the needs of his beast but the compassion of the wicked is cruelty."[11] The bridge to Bergman's thought on blessing was built. The blessing is an expression for a gratitude and reverence for life. What was blessing for Bergman was reverence for Schweitzer. In a reality that gives little weight to the individual, these expressions of reverence seem idealistic and utopian, but they are set forth by men who have a clear vision of reality, whose sensitivity to freedom and justice is highly developed and experienced. There is an awareness of evil and perversity that would make the proud realist blink. These men held forth a fundamental ethical law for which few of us would dare assume responsibility. The sacredness of human life imposes no particular doctrine or cause, but it demands that our actions and attitudes be determined by the moral commitment which the law imposes. We must be conscious of its reality, it conditions our quests and determines our feelings. It is the horizon of our life.

We are continuously in search of the meaning of religion which is, for us, a way to God. This meaning does not only embrace a way to Him, but also His movement toward us. From these movements arise the questions of the meaning of our lives. "What value is to be ascribed to our life? What am I in the world? What is my purpose in it? What may I hope for in the world? I do not want to consider my existence merely as one which constitutes the universe, but as a life which has a value, if I comprehend it and live it according to true knowledge."[12]

---

[9] Albert Schweitzer, *The Philosophy of Civilization* (Tallahassee, University Press of Florida, 1981), 8.
[10] Albert Schweitzer, *Was Sollen Wir Tun?*, 35.
[11] "Proverbs 12:10." (Philadelphia, Jewish Publication Society, 1985).
[12] Albert Schweitzer, *Christianity and the Religions of the World*, cited in *Albert Schweitzer, an Anthology* (Boston, Beacon Press, 1967), 210.

There are the questions and concerns of Schweitzer, but in them we find our questions which we pose and for which we find few responses. Creeds and articles of faith do not help. We need a way to find a sense of belonging to our fellow man and to our world that is more than societal. We need to know that the divine depends upon us, that what we do adds to His creation, and to Him we bring that moral quality of reverence that restores the sacred to creation. We need to know that what we do is a blessing, an "increment and increase" of the human reality. We are enhanced in our being when we treat the creation as a gift which has been given to us through the divine goodness. The creation is His and in our belonging to it we assume a responsibility for it. From this sense of belonging we develop our morality. The self has meaning only when it comprehends its servanthood. We give thanks for what we receive and for the capacity to realize our potentiality. In other words, there was great intelligence embodied in those terms, potentiality and actuality. Where they are lost we become chaotically individualistic. They belong to a natural process which we believe is sacred.

We believe that the divine blessing brings man into relationship with God. Bergman quoted these remarks from Jacob Rosenheim: "The benediction leads to an expression of an entirely new relationship of Man towards God. The will of God is directed to a work on earth, a great work, which will unfold in the course of the ages. Now the conscious cooperation of Man in the divine work on earth, cooperation in the realization of God's aim in the course of civilization – this is the meaning of the benediction recited to God."[13]

We come to the realization that there is a profound difference between a sacred and profane relationship to creation. The sacred relationship implies the recognition of man's cooperation in the work of creation. What we discover and make, our science, art, literature, is not an exclusive human act; it bears in it a divine receptivity. We are aware of the divinity within us that allows us to bring forth works of art and science. The fact is that we are dependent upon a world that was in existence before our recognition of it. We did not create it. We discovered it. In the same way, we do not create ourselves, but we are formed and developed from what was given to us. We lease our talents from the divine. The sacred is embraced when we accept this relationship. The profane, on the other hand, seeks the autonomous. It affirms that man is his own source and law of formation. It rejects the reality of an outside force. It rejects theomorphism. Its work is the highest expression of anthropomorphism. Two opposing visions face

---

[13] "Aphorisms on Jewish Ethical Teaching" in the *S.R. Hirsch Jubilee Volume,* cited in "On Blessings," *Ariel,* 1972, 8-9.

each other as antinomies. We draw consequences from each. Our faith draws us to one or to the other, but we live in both.

Bergman stated clearly the meaning of blessing, of benediction. "The meaning of blessing," he remarked, "lies in the fact it exalts human action – be it ever so small, like the breaking of bread or the drinking of wine – to the level of man's cooperation in the divine fulfillment in the world, in the work of redemption."[14]

What Bergman stressed was the "cosmic holy root" to which all reality belongs. He refused to admit the secularization of created reality which profanes the relationship between man and the world. The profane relation speaks to man, the creator. It is an heroic humanism, a Prometheanism that exalts man's narcissism. The sacred does not lessen man's creativity; it makes it dependent upon the divine. It makes it dependent upon relationships, upon a feeling that there is a creator who has a purpose for his creation. Man knows a reverence for life, he knows that he seeks to find, through that reverence, a way to God. The creation becomes man's raw material when he acknowledges that it belongs to him alone to befoul or to preserve it, to respect or to be arbitrary toward it. Man must either accept that it is from God that he is nourished, or that it is from himself that he determines his validity and purpose.

When we secularize the nexus between man and his world, we tear it away from what Bergman called its "cosmic holy root." "The benediction," he said, "rights the wrong restoring the primary relationship."[15] The benediction is the acknowledgement we make for the goodness of creation. This feeling and recognition that the earth is the Lord's, changes our perspective toward ourselves and toward our obligation to the things around us. What is right or wrong does not depend upon what is pleasing or displeasing, advantageous or disadvantageous, but what is required of us by the creation. What is demanded of us is fundamental and determining. It is not our pleasure but His will. How do we advance and improve the quality of life about us? Schweitzer was clear and simple in his projection of our task. He said, "We must reflect together about the meaning of life, we must strive together to attain to a theory of the universe affirmative of the world and of life, in which the impulse to action which we experience as a necessary and valuable element of our being may find justification, orientation, clarity and depth, and thus become capable of formulating, and of acting on definite ideals of civilization, inspired by the spirit of true humanitarianism."[16]

---

[14] Hugo Bergman, "On Blessings," 8.
[15] *Ibid.*
[16] Albert Schweitzer, *The Philosophy of Civilization*, 64.

From Theory to Practice 121

This may be a voice in the wind, but can the philosopher avoid his calling? His is the voice of the ideal, in him is the courage of its realization. We feel lost finding no being whose action and call bring forth the commitment and faith which each of us should have. We feel lost when no one enumerates it for us.

We remember with pleasure, and a sense of nobility, the faith of Kant in universal peace. We believe his call has become reality. War remains for us unthinkable. We see how desirous the great powers are to contain local conflicts. Nations find their domestic problems of greater importance than foreign ambition and conflict. The production of consumer goods is more valued than military hardware. We struggle for arms reduction and find it more and more necessary to fight against pollution and the death of life in our environment. Kant had told us in *Perpetual Peace* that "if it is a duty to bring about in reality a state of public right (albeit by an intimate process of gradual approximation), and if there are also good grounds for hoping that we shall succeed, then it is not just an empty idea that perpetual peace will eventually replace what have hitherto been wrongly called peace treaties. On the contrary, it is a task which, as solutions are gradually found, constantly draws nearer to fulfillment, for we may hope that the periods within which equal amounts of progress are made will become progressively shorter."[17]

The philosophical heritage belongs to this critical idealism. It does not belong to an idealism that lacks the sense of the heteronomous. When we are aware that our moral development is intimately linked to our responsibility for the creation, we remain outside the sphere of self-intoxication that divorces man from the purpose of God, the reverence for life, and blessing for its goodness.

We understand that our moral development belongs to our sensitivity for the gifts that have been bestowed upon us. Moral life is developed from a sense of appreciation and gratitude. It belongs more to our need to be receptive than to our exaltation of the self. In fact, it is through receptivity that the self finds the fullness of its capacities. In relationships, and not in the splendors of isolation does man find the realization of his creative potentialities. Man discovers the depths of his person through the healing that comes to him in and through the other. We recognize in the other the source of the self. There must always be another to whom we express gratitude. We should also be the other to whom gratitude is given. Bergman cited a well-known verse of the Talmud to clarify his thought. The Talmud (T.B. Berakhot 35b) stated, "If

---

[17]Immanuel Kant, *Perpetual Peace, A Philosophical Sketch*, in *Kant's Political Writings* (Cambridge, Cambridge University Press, 1970), 130.

a man enjoys anything of the world without a benediction, it is as though he robbed the Holy One, blessed be He, and the Community of Israel, as it is said: Who so robbeth his father or his mother – now his father means none other than the Holy One blessed be He...and his mother is none other than the Community of Israel."[18]

What these verses tell us belongs to a question that must precede their prudence and their insights. Schweitzer enunciated it at the end of his book on Kant's *Philosophy of Religion* (1899). "How is the education of the moral personality possible?"[19] Although the solution to the problem was beyond the scope of Schweitzer's work, he made the following important observation: "The moral personality is the result of a moral development which is present in the moral condition of actions in view of their natural coherence. Moral development has a greater possibility in the moral community. The concept of the highest good as the achieved moral community, is realized to the degree that we create the possibility of the moral worth of human relationships."[20]

What Schweitzer pointed to in philosophical language was for us fundamental. The development of the moral person within the individual depends upon the practical involvement of each of us. The question of morality emerges from our critical attitude toward what we are doing, and the meaning of our actions for others and for ourselves, for the world in all its living dimensions. Morality proceeds from involvement and critical experience. The teleological question lies at the basis of a truthful morality. For what end do we affirm or reject an action? When the teleological question is no longer considered, we lose the reality of the divine creator and the purposefulness of creation. The education of the moral personality is the preparation.

The world and man are not only advanced by what we do from our autonomous creativity, but from the greater power we draw into the world through our strength and courage to receive the divine, to have influence on the divine realization. In us there is not only autonomous power for self-realization, but spiritual powers which on different levels, through different activities, realize in the world the divine light, the light of eternity. We activate the "cosmic root of holiness" bringing toward each other the secular and the sacred. We recognize in ourselves moral cosmic forces from which we often retreat, and from which we separated when we lost the courage and strength to believe that God is in some

---

[18] Hugo Bergman, "On Blessings," 10.
[19] Albert Schweitzer. *Die Religionsphilosophie Kants, Von der Kritik der Reinen Vernunft bis zur Religion innerhalb der Grenzen der blossen Vernunft* (Hildesheim, Georg Olms Verlag, 1974), 322.
[20] *Ibid.*, 322-323.

way dependent upon us. This dependence seems shattering to us because we have accustomed ourselves to seek in Him the force we do not find within ourselves. There is, however, a higher capacity in us that makes the divine-human drama so intense and embracing. There is in us a capacity that moves the divine, that brings Him closer to His world and us closer to Him. This is not a problem of knowledge. It is not a cosmic drama. This is a drama and it is significant because it is moral. The moral quality of life has to be enhanced and deepened, that reverence for life substantiated and intensified. We become more intensely involved in the life around us. We are responsible for it and bless its goodness. We add and increase the relationship to the sensitivity to pain in man and mankind, to the experience of daily existence and the need to bring God closer to His creation.

Schweitzer remarked that "the man who does not recognize that sense of elevation which we experience when the wonderful light of the Ought to Help, the *Helfen Duerfen*, fills the ugly night of the "must destroy," *das Zerstoerenmuessen*, does not know how rich life can be."[21]

This cultivation of moral sensitivity linked Bergman to Schweitzer and brought forth in Cassirer a rare admiration. Cassirer admitted the failure of his own scholastic philosophy when he confronted the personality of Schweitzer. Cassirer remarked that "we have all too frequently lost sight of the true connection of philosophy with the world."[22]

This connection between philosophy and the world is the abiding Socratic-Aristotelian heritage. In Schweitzer and Bergman, the connection was intimate and profound. Bergman was truly the "Nestor of Jewish philosophers." His life embodied that same reverence for life that moved and commanded Schweitzer. He was addicted to the Ideal, and in the depths of the night, he refused to surrender its light to the encompassing darkness. These men possessed the faith of reason. With this force they opposed the doubter of the ideal. They were believers in the future, and in the efficacy of hope. They knew they were divine servants, whose lives expressed a servanthood. They also believed that they were affecting God and that He depended upon their strength and courage. Philosophers are men and women of conviction and commitment. Socrates carried his daemon to remind him of what had to be done. Every philosopher inherits it from him. Cassirer realized the futility of scholastic philosophy to accomplish the true work of philosophy. We admired in Schweitzer what he could never do, but

---

[21]Albert Schweitzer, *Was Sollen Wir Tun?*, 51.
[22]Ernst Cassirer, "The Concept of Philosophy" in *Symbol, Myth, and Culture*, 60.

could appreciate. We admire Cassirer for his struggle against the myth, for his loyalty to the ethical.

The last remark belongs to Toni Cassirer. She said, "I had been married to a philosopher for thirty years and I was never able to feel at ease with philosophical language. In fact, I carried out an inner struggle against it. Now there is a man (Schweitzer) standing before me whose quality I never doubted, and he did not use this language."[23] We could repeat this story and substitute the name of Bergman.

This remarkable quality of using straightforward, albeit profound, expressions was possessed by Bergman. It is for this reason that these men were the Nestors of our age.

---

[23]Toni Cassirer, *Mein Leben mit Ernst Cassirer*, 236.

10

A Spiritual Encounter

Simone Weil found an admirer in Hugo Bergman. This was a strange and fascinating spiritual encounter. A believing philosopher was deeply moved by a Jewish-born woman whose love of Christianity relegates her thoughts about Judaism to minor and negative generalizations. She knows little and wants to know less of her family's faith. She loved Jesus, she disdained the creation, and she sought redemption from a world condemned to death. What brought Bergman to her side, to a deep respect for her faith, and to several writings about her in both Hebrew and German, is the subject of this chapter. The encounter tells us much about the rare qualities of Bergman's life and thought. His thinking was the last great expression of religious humanism, of the love of the universal and the invisible. He embraced every manifestation of the universal word that sensitivity and appreciation. The universalism that lived in Hebraism was Bergman's finest achievement. His appreciation of Simone Weil revealed the purity of his thought.

Simone Weil was born on February 3, 1909, in Paris, her father, Dr. Bernard Weil in Strasbourg on April 7, 1872, and her mother, Selma Reinherz, in Rostov-on Dov, in 1879. "The Reinherzes," Simone Petrément tells us, "were a cultured, musical and artistic family. Adolphe Reinherz (Selma's father) was a poet; he wrote poetry in Hebrew that was said to be beautiful; and he also collected books in Hebrew."[1]

The Jewishness of Simone's father was marked and prevalent. Her paternal grandmother was "a pious Jew." When she visited her son "she would follow Mme. Weil to the kitchen to make sure that she did not

---

[1] Simone Petrément, *Simone Weil, A Life* (New York, Schocken Books, 1976), 4.

cook anything contrary to Jewish dietary laws."[2] This background shows that there was no absence of Jewish piety, tradition and awareness, but it did not make a serious impression on Simone. Her life was conditioned by her work at the Lycée Henri IV and the École Normale. At Henri IV, she found the philosopher Alain. His influence was abiding. She learned Greek and discovered a love for Plato. She found Athens and lost Jerusalem.

What brought Bergman to the thought of this extraordinary woman? The first entrance in his diary about Simone was April 13, 1951. She had died in 1943. Bergman reported a conversation which he had with his friend, the philosopher Martin Buber. "We spoke about Simone Weil and converts. Buber said that he could not imagine a Jew sincerely believing in the Trinity. 'Attributes,' yes, but Persons! I replied that the distinction did not seem to me to be great, but rather a distinction of words."[3]

We note immediately the difference in attitudes between Buber and Bergman. Buber's rejection is what we would expect: the Jew has always found it difficult to approach the Cross and experience the sufferings of Jesus. He does not comprehend the Christ. This is an experience from which the Jew is not only estranged, but to which he is a stranger. He believes he has no possibility of a relationship or communication with the Cross. Bergman might have had the same feelings, but he found in Simone's personality a faith, something that surpasses the problem of conversion and the nature of the Trinity. It was Bergman's peculiar and remarkable quality that he could find in the varied forms of religious expressions vehicles of the one unique religious truth. In fact, we may say, that his religious thinking showed the possibility of grasping in every historical religious manifestation a "spark," a "hint," a "mark" of divine revelation.

In July and August of 1952, Bergman read two books of Simone Weil, *Waiting on God* and *The Need for Roots*. The latter, he mentioned, he was rereading. After noting his rereading of *The Need for Roots, Prelude to a Declaration of Duties Towards Mankind,* Bergman made the following commentary: "Today man can call himself educated (*kultiviert*) without a concept of man's fate. There is no other salvation for mankind than the remaining island of the past. The future gives us nothing. We must give to it and have nothing other to give to it than the treasures of the past as we have assimilated them."[4]

---

[2]*Ibid.*, 3.
[3]Hugo Bergman, *Tagebuecher & Briefe*, 4/13/15 article "Simone Weil" in *Mitteilungsblatt* 10 October, 1952, 39/40.
[4]*Ibid.*, 8/4/52.

Bergman's remarks were inspired by what he had read. Simone spoke of obligations in human affairs. She noted that "there exists an obligation towards every human being, without any other recognition of such obligation on the part of the individual concerned.... Duty towards the human being as such – that alone is eternal."[5]

This concern for the individual had deep religious roots. Whatever we say about the tradition is of lesser value than the identity of thinking and doing, the realization that the engaged philosopher is the true philosopher. He is the philosopher of values, the searcher for truth, the man of commitment.

The reading of Simone's works, the intimate tie she created between her thinking and doing draws every human being closer to her. Her friend, Father Perrin, included in *Waiting for God*, a deeply moving letter of Simone that forcefully expressed her life. She spoke of the Church and her inability to enter it. She noted that "so many things exist outside it, so many things that I love and do not want to give up, so many things that God loves, otherwise they would not be in existence.... I should like to draw your attention to one point. It is that there is an absolutely insurmountable obstacle to the incarnation of Christianity. It is the use of the two little words *'anathema sit'*.... I remain with all these things that cannot enter the Church.... I remain with them all the more because my own intelligence is numbered among them.... The proper function of the intelligence demands total freedom."[6]

If the philosopher has a deep sensitivity to what is occurring around him, and if he is driven by his devotion to truth, he finds it difficult to be bound by the strictures of an historical faith. This can be stated paradoxically. The believer is bound to the teachings of the faith, but in a way that enhances his freedom and capacity to find a knowledge which encompasses both his faith and reason. Bergman sought harmony between believer and thinker. He dedicated his writing to these types and lived among them. Simone went beyond the desire of the thinker to know. Her life and thought were experiences which could be received only by those who felt deeply her love and her capacity for pain and sacrifice. Bergman loved the faith of this Jewish woman and felt deeply the sacrifice she knew she had to make for the love of God. She was a sacrificial lamb in whom all mankind suffered.

In a letter to a disciple and friend, Luise Hermann, Bergman expressed his feelings about Simone. He wrote, "I am deeply absorbed

---

[5]Simone Weil, *The Need for Roots: Prelude to a Declaration of Duties Towards Mankind*. (London, Ark Paperback, 1987) 4-5. Bergman apparently read these books in French. French edition appeared in 1949.
[6]Simone Petrément, *Simone Weil, A Life*, 465.

in a wonderful work. I will write for a Journal a work on Simone Weil and it should be finished on the 15th of August, although it probably won't be. The reading of the writings of this great woman is an extraordinary experience. I am startled by this faith in God that is so deeply and intimately bound to an unusual intelligence, even in practical political things. The extent of her reading is overwhelming. She died so young. She hated her Judaism like death or perhaps, more than death, because she loved death and longed for it. All this is frightfully upsetting...."[7]

Bergman was the great listener. He believed in the voice of tradition, the need to listen to God's word. He taught those near to him how to listen, in the writings of others, to the hints of divinity. He taught us to listen to what lay hidden in the texts. He forced us not only to see what was external but what spoke through the internal. Hearing was a gift, a grace, that had to be developed. It required patience and cultivation. The hearer was an initiate to myth and mystery. He knew that behind the word was the Word, a language behind languages. The sound, the form, the sense, are paths from language to language. Learning to listen demands the education of the soul, a sensitivity to those rumors and signs that only spiritual cultivation could create.

On the 12th of August, Bergman made this entry into his diary, "I read again in Simone Weil and stenographed the chapter on gravity and grace. It should be short in terms of the whole essay. I am not yet clear about the direction of my critique, because the problem, *die Sache selbst*, is not clear to me. I can follow Thibon and say that it is a way to God like so many others, but perhaps, one must take a fundamental position to her denial of the world and the history of progress. Isaiah said that death will be swallowed up. With her death brings the person to God, and consequently misery."[8]

Bergman would not take a negative position toward Simone's gnosticism, the belief that God had withdrawn from the world. He remained open to it, knowing that it was comprehended in Judaism. He struggled to understand it in her thought and faith. It was impossible for Bergman to be opposed to a believer he admired. He would rather lay a limitation upon himself than declare Simone wrong. In fact, right and wrong in these questions had little meaning for him. One had to listen and attempt to comprehend, to wait and with patience hope to find the strength for a deeper and redeeming knowledge whose foundation was given, but denied in its fullness to any one man. "We are vessels with

---

[7]Hugo Bergman, *Tagebuecher*, 8/5/52.
[8]*Ibid.*, 8/12/52.

A Spiritual Encounter

one ground" he quoted from Simone, "as long as we do not know that we have one ground."[9]

Simone seemed never to have left Bergman's thoughts. He believed her religious commitment to be truthful and he continued to speak and write about her. He mentioned that his article about her in the Hebrew Encyclopedia, was derived previously from her book *Oppression and Liberty* (1955). On May 3rd, Bergman reported that he had finished his article on Simone Weil for the Encyclopedia. He discovered some parallels between the Sermon of Paneloux in Camus's *The Plague* and Simone's gnosticism. He said, "This frightful thought is to see from the beginning in the creation a minus, all the misery in creation as primordially given with the creation. This is a denial of God's calling for redemption and recovery. Salvation is nothing other than the destruction of the world. There is no hope for a redeemed world. All this is frightful, however unbelievably courageous it may be.... According to Simone Weil, Abraham must lead his son to the sacrifice as something self-understood. The world must go the same way even if it would believe that God had not given the command. God has nothing to say in this world. It belongs to 'Oppression,' to evil.... Who would want to live in such a world?"[10]

Another question can be posed. Is there a world in which God is present? This and others are questions we cannot escape. Bergman once remarked that "we must search everywhere because everywhere something can be found *(Wir muessen ueberall suchen, denn ueberall kann etwas gefunden werden)."*[11]

We do not surrender one question to another, but attempt to comprehend how they evoke each other and must live with each other. Gnosticism has been with us for two centuries and will remain with us as long as men are religiously moved. It remains because it is a fundamental religious commitment. It cannot be refuted without doing violence to religious reality.

Simone's biographer, Petrément, is the leading scholar of gnosticism. Her book, *Le Dieu Séparé* (1984), is the source of much that we know of gnosticism. In her biography of Simone, she remarked that "she (Simone) does not in any way wish to obliterate God but on the contrary, wants to define him by a description that, in her view, is essential to the idea of the true God. For her, two things are essential to this idea: one is

---

[9]*Ibid.*, 9/10/52.
[10]*Ibid.*, 5/3/58.
[11]*Ibid.*, 7/10/61.

that God is the Good, and the other, that he is outside the world, at least in a sense."[12]

For a believing Jew, who is so encompassed by the history of Israel, to come to terms with the divine absence, is difficult and perhaps insurmountable. Bergman's question, if answered affirmatively, would reveal how personal and intimate God is to his people, a precious people, a light to the world. The absence of God is the foundation of a distinct human morality. The world is governed by inherent laws which man discovers in nature and in himself. The answer to Cain's question, Am I my brother's keeper?, to Job's suffering and doubts, remain basic human problems. Man finds himself in the world without a divinely moral code, and has to develop a human one. He must comprehend the meaning of idolatry and the nature of necessity and freedom. Man is the being who asks about values, who questions the destiny of his species and the quality of his individualism, who creates a history and is subject to its distortion. The world encloses man. Man has no dwelling beyond it.

Bergman's question finds no definitive answer. It is a challenge. No one challenged his own faith more deeply than Simone. She challenged the faith in each of us. It is difficult not to take her thought and life seriously. She raised the question of creation and revelation, of God's presence and absence. Petrément stated that she believed that "for God, creation did not consist in extending, but rather in withdrawing himself. He did not create outside himself beings who did not exist before, thus extending the domain in which to exercise his power. On the contrary, he left outside himself a domain that before was within him and was himself, and in which he no longer intervenes or does so only under certain conditions."[13]

Bergman's confrontation with Simone was an essential instance of his religious experience. It was a moment in his unending search which forces every way to see its limitations. The way is *a* truth in and from which we attempt to live and act. Bergman never wanted to escape the fat that Simone believed in God. She died for Him. The challenge of her death was and is overwhelming. In the depths of his faith, Bergman knew that Simone loved God. He was in awe of her. We must remember that Bergman devoted much of his life to a philosophy of faith in which he sought to encounter modes of religious thinking. Bergman was in search of the faith.

In a diary entry for June 1958, Bergman spoke of his discussion with his Prague colleague Felix Weltsch, about his book, *Religion and Humor*.

---

[12] Simone Petrément, *Simone Weil, A Life*, 494.
[13] *Ibid.*, 496.

The discussion, he said, recalled the thoughts of Simone. In the same entry, Bergman noted the work of his friend, David Flusser, a professor of the New Testament at the Hebrew University. Of Flusser, he commented, "Dr. Flusser taught the students to understand the New Testament as an important challenge in the religious development of Israel and to distinguish between the religion of Jesus and the myth of Christianity."[14]

Bergman continuously sought to overcome what he called the *Ghetto-Angst* toward the New Testament. We mention these facts because they reveal how deeply Bergman was concerned with the divinity in all faiths. He had a remarkable capacity to appreciate and, in a sense, to participate in faiths not his own. He was a searching believer. He was sensitive to the searching of others, but there remained in him a positive skepticism that opened systems, sought clarification and attempted to understand dogmatic attitudes. He refused to allow himself to be a judge, to be insensitive. He wanted to lay before us the possibilities that were part of the conflicting positions and attitudes of every human experience.

Bergman's question about our willingness to live in a world from which God has withdrawn, haunts the problem of creation and the meaning of God's love of his world and man. "By withdrawing," Petrément noted, "God has allowed us to exist; he has done so for the sake of love and so that we ourselves, for the sake of love, can renounce the being he has given us."[15]

This withdrawal has given man the task to seek God beyond the world in which He is no longer present. The love of God forces upon us a 'decreation,' a term that had deep significance for Simone. The more we long to describe what this withdrawal means, the more we are aware that it is in and beyond *our* language. We read through language to a different and new experience, to novel and powerful feelings and devotions. Into this hearing and seeing, Bergman entered with his patience and questioning. He heard Simone. He loved her. There was more in his faith in Israel than she could comprehend or would admit. Only because he was so faithful to Israel, could he appreciate Simone's experience. We approach others with sympathy and sensitivity if we are committed to faith.

It would appear that the more deeply man enters the religious life, the more he grows aware of its paradoxical nature. Nothing was more characteristic of Bergman's life than paradox, his capacity to hear contradiction and to explore antinomies. He loved Kant's antinomies. The singular faith of a dogmatic religion was impossible for him,

---

[14]Hugo Bergman, *Tagebuecher*, 6/1/58.
[15]Simone Petrément, *Simone Weil*, 497.

although he could comprehend it. We find the same characteristic in Simone. Petrément remarked that for Simone "on certain points, contradiction cannot be avoided if one doesn't want to lie to oneself. For her, this fact represents one of the proofs of a transcendent reality. The irreconcilable contradiction between two equally and certainly true affirmations shows us that absolute truth dwells on a higher plane, beyond our reach.... Perhaps there exists a level of thought, or rather, a level of problems, where truth can be expressed only through myth and beauty."[16]

If we try to comprehend the sympathy and admiration that existed between Bergman and Simone's religious life, then we must recognize a few fundamental facts. Bergman had the capacity to receive sensitively the religious attitudes of others. He deeply loved his own faith. His own faith was not a set of fixed rules or the consequence of the contents of some holy books. His fidelity to the tradition was rooted in the search for comprehension and fidelity. He accepted the antinomic quality of human thought because he knew that its violation ended in an absolutism that would become idolatry. Bergman could not, and never would, separate thinking and believing. This was for him the human fate. The believer was the thinker, and the thinker the believer.

In his diaries, Bergman enunciated his personal faith in an entry dated July 10, 1961. "I will begin," he wrote, "with Rosenzweig's concept of revelation. We have no written book that is for us the final authority. We have the I in us. The peculiar human authority is the voice in me. It is necessary to distinguish in me the voice from the small I. This is the great danger and temptation, 'Versuchung' that lies in us: to identify the eternal I and the I in me. Thus, there is no formula for the appeal to an authority. This would transform faith immediately into something heteronomous. Who gives authority to authority? There is nothing else but to hear the inner voice and to do everything to strengthen this authority.... This requires hours of study which become constant habit, a way of life. Seek everywhere, for in all places something can be found. From the perspective of faith it is completely the same whether I draw close to Jewish or non-Jewish greatness.... God allows himself to be found. The holy writings of all religions, the confessions of Santa Theresa, the tales of Rabbi Nachman, the theoretical writings of Rudolf Steiner or of F.D. Ouspensky are all sources of faith."[17]

We read this confession and we are startled by the openness that one religious experience can have for another. We could say that what is

---

[16]*Ibid.*, 498-499.
[17]Hugo Bergman, *Tagebuecher*, 7/10/61.

fundamental is the ground from which I begin. The more it is possible for the believer to be sensitive and sympathetic to other divine manifestations, the more he comprehends his own faith. Bergman's embrace of Simone was possible only because he was a believer, a Jew firmly rooted in his fidelity to Israel. We read Bergman with the feeling that we have only begun to comprehend the religious, that we must separate the latter from the observed, although observance belongs to the religious. Man's capacity to embrace what is different is limited, but limitation does not necessarily become fixation.

Simone reminded us that "those things and ideas that keep masses of men in subjection by exercising force and cruelty, deprives them at once of two vital foods, liberty and obedience, for it is no longer within the power of such masses to accord their inner consent to the authority to which they are subjected.... There are any number of signs showing that the men of our age have now for a long time been starved for obedience. But advantage has been taken of the fact to give them slavery."[18]

Man needs to honor tradition if he is to think. There is a profound emptiness in man that longs for the infinite. God is there for those who are in search of Him. His presence is hidden in His absence. Our world gives us only hints of His presence. We suffer His absence. We are challenged to comprehend the world that has been given to us, and we longed for the goodness that we must find in it. God's goodness is the foundation of our morality. It is the "should be" that confronts being, the infinite that faces and calls to the finite. Man does not escape the antinomic quality of his existence without entering into idolatry. Beyond the antinomies of his life lies the reality of Transcendence. Man needs to ask himself about his destiny. Where is it taking him? Where are the values encompassed in it?

Education begins with the cultivation of questioning. Bergman asked how it is possible to live in a world from which God has withdrawn. He expected no answer. He lived *his* faith knowing that *hers* was also actual. She lived truth as he lived it. He knew and believed that the God of Israel was truth, but he also knew that the truth of this creation could be grasped with Simone's faith in God's withdrawal. Each perspective is a contradiction for human reason, but a source of human freedom.

Bergman's embrace of Simone was rare and beautiful, a religious encounter. It revealed the possibility of a thinker and believer embracing the other. Bergman spoke of ecumenism. He knew that it was possible and actual. He realized that the human experience has just begun to bring forth its encompassing powers. Mankind was not a fixed term, not

---

[18] Simone Weil, *The Need for Roots*, 14.

limited to an ideology, but a vast possibility. We have only hints of this reality. We call them the human spirit. Every manifestation of it yields evidence of its indescribable dimension. We have come to understand that divinity is found in a multitude of religious experiences and places. Bergman remarked that we should search everywhere, in all places something could be found. He offered us a task, but he also revealed to us its actuality in life. He, like Simone, lived his knowledge and faith. There is goodness in the bond and the binding that brings one to the other. In it we find the trust which educates our youth. Bergman's life was its teaching.

11

Faith in the Absence of Conclusions

We begin with an encounter. Much that is valued and significant occurs in the mystery of the moment. This short conversation took place in October of 1961. Hugo Bergman asked Jean Sulzberger, a close friend, a personal question, "I asked her what are my negative qualities? She replied, You have no faults. When I pressed her, she said, my faults are that I jump from one school to another. I said to her that it was not true. All these schools were for me the struggle to break down the walls."[1] This simple story indicates a direction which Bergman followed through the course of his life. In fact, the encounter points both forwards and backwards. The path of life that he followed drove him deeper into the depths of his own faith and to visions of ways, followed by men of faith, which lead to the oneness of God. These ways belonged to individuals rather than to institutions. We feel more of the Protestant than the Catholic in emphasis and feeling. The imagination is more Kantian and Fichtean than Platonic. Bergman lived in a world of individuals and communities and rarely expressed a sympathy for the Idea of Church. Although he spoke of community, we never sense its eternal truth, but rather its empirical reality. But there is always the presence of God and the continuing human response that this presence elicits. Bergman reminded us that "we should so live our life that it is truly ours but linked to the oneness of God."[2]

When we speak of "our" God, we know that He is the God of all men. Here we touch that precious and necessary dialectic that remained at the heart of Bergman's life: the relationship of universality and individuality, of God and man. It is far easier to speak of this dialectic than to live it. This search for that universality that never compromised

---
[1] *Tagebuecher & Briefe*, 10/11/61.
[2] *Ibid.*, 10/23/50.

the individuality of faith, brought Bergman many periods of agonizing doubt. He tried to encompass a world of thought and ways of belief, to comprehend in each way a truth that was formulated differently from his own, to see the positive when he felt the reality of the negative, to cultivate that sympathy which should not be confused with sentimentality. It would have been easier to proclaim a doctrine and a belief to the world, to speak of it time and time again, and to structure it in innumerable articles and books and then to become known as its foremost exponent. Bergman refused this approach. The powers of his syncretistic mind drove him from level to level of spiritual life, and the best that he could do would be to elucidate the journey that he voluntarily and necessarily had to take. He was a thinker who moved deeply into his individuality, and, at the moment, moved toward that universality that he deeply loved and which commanded his life. Love was his path to the immortality which he deeply yearned for.

In the later conversation with Bergman, Jean Sulzberger explained her remarks more fully. She clarified for Bergman the expression, "Grace without power."

Bergman recorded Jean's words, "I (Bergman) have nothing with which to identify myself, and consequently I fragment my power in things that are not my own. I do not have my own things."[3] Bergman accepted the judgment as severe but justified. In response, he said, "I cannot identify myself with anything that is not my life and is a foundation for my being."[4] We have often cited these words because they are the sources of strength and weakness. The failure of Bergman to identify himself with attitudes and beliefs is, in fact, untrue, but identification for him meant development and change, not fixity. There could be no fixed identification with any human thought or reality, and with God we could hardly speak of identification. We live in an unfinished universe from which new natural and spiritual forms are always developing. Man's awareness is forever in change and we cannot declare that what is known at a particular moment is not in reality, only the foundation for a new and yet unexplored meaning and interpretation. A life linked to God never frees the mortal from the depths of mortality, from its differentiation from the immortal. If love carries us from one to the other, it never binds us in such a way that we lose the sense of distinction and individuality.

Bergman believed that every moment of reality was a passage to and a message from a higher realm. Men hold on to what they have because they fear the unknown quality of the journey to higher realms. Great

---

[3] *Ibid.*, 10/1/64.
[4] *Ibid.*

Faith in the Absence of Conclusions

love is the courage to go forward, to leave the world of fixed forms for higher realities. Bergman did not have his own things in the sense that what he believed and understood remained filled with possibilities that drove his imagination beyond the security of fixed social, political and religious forms. From the present he moved toward the visions of the future which would bring with them the Messianic mankind he so deeply loved. Bergman, like Abraham, was always on a journey, leaving one land for another.

Bergman wandered the earth in search of ideas and beliefs which would awaken in him and in others a profounder sense of man's struggle to be free of the ignorance that surrounds him in all directions. In 1947, he began to read the spectacular works of one of India's greatest contemporary philosophers, Sri Aurobindo (1872-1950). Of these beginnings, Bergman remarked, "Through the writings of Sri Aurobindo that I have just begun to read, I have new perspective for a more fundamental metaphysical orientation. I know as yet much too little of it to say whether it will be a lasting advancement or, after some time, I will put it down. In any case, in the little I have read in the involution and revolution, the hope for a new mankind there lies a concreteness of metaphysical ideas. They do not float in the clouds, but are bound to reality."[5]

With his reading of Aurobindo, there began a period of thought which lasted till his death in 1975. In 1947, Bergman traveled to India as chairman of a delegation to a Pan Asian conference to which the Hebrew University was invited. The trip was of vital significance for him. it fed his openness. It was a new moment in his spiritual life. We illustrate this with an odd but characteristic incident in Delhi. Bergman met a man at his hotel who had come to tell him about his presence in the city and at a divine service. Bergman listened to him, another might probably have turned him away as a quack. What he told Bergman enchanted him. Bergman knew how to listen. He said to Bergman that "the goal of man is to be freed from the wheel of reincarnation. Man alone brings about his Karma in the next incarnation. If he redeems himself, he returns to God. God does not affect the fate of man; man affects his own fate. These remarks excited me very much; above all, his firm insistence that man, and he alone, forged his own fate and no divine influence should be expected. This is an outlook that is indeed heroic, but God is then totally superficial for the world."[6]

If we seek in Sri Aurobindo what would attract Bergman, we would find in his major work, *The Life Divine*, a spirituality that was

---
[5] *Ibid.*, 1/9/47.
[6] *Ibid.*, 3/19/47.

fundamental for his faith in a new mankind. Bergman was a thinker who thought with others, who sought the spiritual partnership that he needed to confirm his own thought, to help him seek ways toward new experiences. He sought the conversation in which he could expand his thinking. He needed to hear the experiences of others. He knew that man alone was incomplete, and that every attempt to create philosophy without dialogue was for him an impossibility. He thought less like Spinoza or Hegel, and more like William James. He believed deeply in the need for spiritual guidance. He was a philosopher for whom receptivity was more vital than spontaneity. He was neither a system builder nor a disciple; he was a poet of insights, of vignettes and experiences. He was a writer of diaries and letters. He found in other men ways of the spirit that were not his, but were significant for his experiences. He found richness in dependency. He lived less through what was similar to him than what was different from him. His spiritual guides changed often, not because they were no longer meaningful, but because he had become open to new and novel possibilities that had now been revealed to him. His relationship with friends like Martin Buber, Gershom Scholem, Robert and Felix Weltsch, remained constant but they never absorbed the power of his searching, nor could they embrace his inexhaustible curiosity and comprehension. In his need for dialogue and spiritual companionship, he remained like James a deeply lonely soul. He never enjoyed that security which came with the conviction that the categories of reasonable life had been found, and that reason had found them sufficient for the means and purpose of rational human life.

Bergman lived with agonizing doubts. He plunged deeper and deeper into Jewish ritual, but this always remained a two-way movement. He moved toward others of vastly different faith with equal intensity and love. He was a man of paradoxes and opposites whose richness of spirit was astounding. We ask about Sri Aurobindo and *The Life Divine* and we realize that Bergman could not avoid being fascinated by his thought. Sri Aurobindo in the twenty-fourth chapter of *The Life Divine*, stated that "spirituality is in its essence an awakening to inner reality of our being, to a spirit, self, soul, which is other than our mind, life and body, an inner aspiration to know, to feel, to be that, to enter into contact with the greater Reality beyond and pervading the universe which inhabits also our own being, to be in communication with it and union with it, and a turning, a conversion, a transformation of our whole being, as a result of the aspiration, the contact, the union, a growth or making into a new becoming or new being, a new self, a new nature."[7] We speak here of ideas that were always precious to Bergman; we speak

---

[7] *The Divine Life* (Pondicherry, Sri Aurobindo-Ashram, 1973), 857.

Faith in the Absence of Conclusions

of transformation, turning, awakening, growth. This is the vocabulary of those who know that the spiritual foods come from above and rarely from around us. Bergman never forgot Kafka's tale, "The Investigation of a Dog."

Bergman was always present to the immediate problems of his historical situation. He could travel to India and read their holy books and meet their thinkers, but the problems of Israel were always utmost in his thought. Sri Aurobindo could say that "you are surely mistaken in thinking that I said that we work spiritually for the relief of the poor. I have never done that. My work is not to intervene in social matters within the frame of the present humanity, but to bring down a higher spiritual power of a higher character which will make a radical change in the earth-consciousness."[8] But Bergman had another approach which he put forth in the work of "The Sanctification of the Holy Name." In his life effort he struggled to find the reality for this sanctification in a world of conflict and irreconcilable oppositions. Where and how Bergman asked, is this sanctification a human reality, where does it find its realization and what are the efforts that make it possible? Bergman remarked in 1967 that "we should not become the sacrifice of our victory. We should not allow ourselves to be ruled by a psychology of conquest. In your hands lies the fate of the historical hour, through your relationship you will decide, through your rapport with man, above all with the Arabs, with the Arab people, whether Zionism is a nationalism like that of other peoples or whether also today we should say: Zionism is the sanctification of the Holy Name." Bergman's remarks went further and he expressed a belief that never wavered, but which brought him pain and disillusionment. He noted the sixty-seven war contained a miracle "if we would express it religiously. We can say that God has saved our small state and with it the possibility for sanctification of his Name in this state, to make it the center point of mankind not through strength, but through His Spirit."[9]

Bergman was moved by his belief in God, in the presence of the divine reality and His effects in history. He was asked by a visiting Rabbi from Boston if "we could have a humanistic religion and yet be true to the tradition." He found an answer difficult; he found all answers difficult, but finally he hesitantly said that "for me, the most important thing is to believe in a higher world that leads us, and which we have sinned against in our youth because we have clouded our view of the above, and that for me is most important. I concluded with an appeal for

---

[8] *Sri Aurobindo on Himself* (Pondicherry, Sri Aurobindo-Ashram, 1972), 151.
[9] *Briefe & Tagebuecher*, (Summer, 1967). The original article was published in *Vom Judentum* (Prague, Bar-Kochba, 1914).

an ecumenical dialogue, the necessity to learn from it and the great possibility for *Jerusalem* in this regard."[10] We feel that Bergman's thought is as much inspired as it is developed and formed. He found it difficult to provide definitions and formulae for others. This refusal to give more than preliminary answers did not hide indecision and disorder, but revealed Plato's similar thoughts about the inadequacies of the written text. Bergman knew that his thought often defied the preciseness afforded to the sciences, or those who had decided to limit their thoughts to a pattern of ideas or a fixed logical system. Bergman never wanted the listener to believe in the finality of his remarks. In the spiritual realm no human vocabulary could capture the workings of the divine spirit and those who make the effort betray its truth.

Religions cannot be compared; they are living organisms and the forms which they develop belong intimately to their spiritual needs and their primordial revelation. Bergman, in this sense, found great support in Frithjof Schuon whose *Transcendental Unity of Religions*, he greatly admired. When in 1955, he was asked by the newspaper *Maariv* what were the three most important books he had to read that year, he replied, *The Zohar*, Romano Guardini's *Vorschule des Gebetes* (The Pre-School of Prayer) and Schuon's *The Transcendental Unity of Religions*. This is an odd and distinct list, but for Bergman a normal one: Jewish Mysticism, a Catholic theologian's discussion of prayer and a Sufi who lived in Lausanne and whom Bergman visited in 1957.

The world had many spiritual leaders and Bergman sought them either in their dwellings or through their books. He knew that they had something to offer him, and it was their messages that he wanted to hear. He had no desire to be their disciple, but he enjoyed their friendship, their letters and their works. He created about him a community of believers who shared with each other the values and visions that they had discovered in their lives. Bergman found it sinful not to communicate with them. No man embodied the spirit; men shared the Word and each becomes a teacher and listener of the other. Without external organization, a living community of men devoted to the Spirit formed itself naturally into a tranquil, unseen community of believers in the unity of the Word – its embrace of what is mortal and immortal, what is finite and infinite.

Schuon had set forth the idea that each religion is an organic whole. He stated that "a religion is an integral whole comparable to a living organism that develops according to necessary and exact laws; one might therefore call it a spiritual organism, or a social one in its most outward aspect. In any case, it is an organism and not a construction of arbitrary

---

[10]*Ibid.*, 7/26/71.

Faith in the Absence of Conclusions

conventions; one cannot therefore legitimately consider the constituent elements of a religion independently of their inward unity, as if one were concerned with a mere collection of facts."[11]

We note with either pleasure or despair that Bergman found no resting place in thought or in religious practice. Often he would state his beliefs but we are aware that their manifestation and implications took him in many directions. He thought through the consequences of beliefs he found in others, he allowed them to become his guides, but he remained restless and hesitant in his acceptance and devotion. He knew only the reality of divine attachment. The richness of the human experience and the possibilities that it contained, were overwhelming for him. The spirit took on so many forms and expressions that no man could be honest with himself and declare that he had become the embodiment of it. Prophets could speak its words, although they burned their lips, and philosophers, in their pride, could attempt to be spokesmen, but when it was revealed the believer knew that he was incapable of being its manifestation. The human experience trembles in its inadequacies and suffers in its attempts to be loyal to spiritual separation. With the most extensive and rich imagination man feels his limitations, the fate of his mortality.

In a moving and deeply characteristic diary entry, Bergman, two years before his death in 1975, spoke of his insatiable desire to read and think. "If I may only find the time to read all that I want and should read! The collected essays of Steiner, from his pre-anthroposophic time, lies here unread for several years. How deeply I loved many of them when they appeared."[12] This is the sadness of a scholar, or the continuity of an attitude that lay in him for a lifetime, a fate of character and an indispensable destiny. He loved Rudolf Steiner's refusal to accept the duality between sense perception and spiritual life. Steiner, in his autobiography, made it clear that in his book *Philosophy of Freedom*, he sought to show "that no unknown lies *behind* the sense-world, but that *within* it lies the spiritual. And as to the domain of human ideas, I sought to show that these have their existence in that spiritual world. The essential nature of the spiritual world, therefore, is hidden from human consciousness only *so long as* the mind perceives by means of the senses *alone*. When, in addition to sense-perception, ideas also are experienced, the sense-world, in its objective being, is embraced within consciousness. Knowing does not consist in a mirroring of something possessing essential being, but the soul's living entrance into this reality of being.

---

[11]*The Transcendental Unity of Religions* (New York, Harper & Row, 1975), 101.
[12]*Tagebuecher & Briefe*, 2/8/73.

Within consciousness occurs that advance from the still unreal sense-world to its essential reality."[13]

Steiner had been a spiritual companion to Bergman throughout his life. The search for an understanding of man follows many ways, but it is essential to explore that entrance of the soul into the reality of being. This is an endless journey of revelation and spiritual subtlety and it was one that Bergman never ceased to pursue. He showed mankind that the journey of the soul to higher realms of being is endless. Like Diotima, he was capable of teaching us to take the first steps and draw apart the first of the veils, but only God knows how we proceed from that moment on. Bergman always left much to the yet to be decided.

Bergman's views took on very concrete forms. He and Nathan Rotenstreich had finished their translation of Kant's *Eternal Peace*. Bergman noted the fact that they had agreed to dedicate the book to the idea of an understanding between Jews and Arabs. "It is a great joy for me," Bergman remarked, "that Nathan agreed to this proposal."[14] This was a rich symbol and statesmen could find in these philosophic men a dedication to peace and public debate that was rare and precious in a world of conflict. It was more than a gesture of the philosophical life; it was the enhancement of the light from which Plato knew our eyes found their time light. We often face the criticism that Bergman's ideas had little to do with the power-political reality about him, but the philosopher never understood his message to be only an understanding of the world around him, a mirroring of its reality. He sought the truth that lay behind the phenomena which he encountered in his daily existence. He responded to it with a new message which did not always come forth and reveal its contents. Like the parable "The Imperial Message" of Franz Kafka, Bergman knew that a message had been given to mankind and told to a messenger who tried but knew that he would never reach mankind. This paradox of revelation and silence has always plagued the believer. Bergman lived the paradoxical truth of silence and revelation. he lived in this "between."

Men of deep religious conviction and vision often find it difficult to advise those who came to them for help and advice. Bergman was deeply dependent upon others for inspiration and guidance, but the latter became sources of great creativity. They filled a need that lay at the foundation of his work. He created from dialogue and conversation. The spirit dwelt in the reality of the "between." It was neither present in the "I" nor in the "you." Each moment of the dialogue proved insufficient and incapable of revelation. The mystery emerged in that

---

[13]*The Course of My Life* (New York, Anthoposophic Press, 1951), 181-182.
[14]*Tagebuecher & Briefe*, 6/7/73.

Faith in the Absence of Conclusions

peculiar place which is the ground of both "I" and "you." This foundation is neither given nor created; it comes about with explanation and force. It is there and not there; its presence and its absence is its reality. It is not a bridge which we can build, nor a path we can put forth. The reality of the "between" depends upon the intensity of the relationship between the moments of the dialogue. Dialogue is as rare as talk is common. Dialogue endures but also fades away. It comes and it goes, it separates but it does not often return and given new forms. Dialogue is precious, but fickle; it appears secure; but it is fleeting. Bergman knew its mystery and when others came to see him, he offered little dialogue. Everything depended upon the consequences of the conversation. Everything depended upon God's will. We illustrate this with a story of a man who came to see about details for some philosophical books he wanted to read. Bergman seemed convinced that the man was plagued with religious doubt and he saw immediately that he could not help him. "The modern philosopher would only confuse him because he is, in fact, only a catalogue of possible points of view. I advised him to read Plato's *Republic* and *The Confessions* of Augustine. I didn't dare to name Kant."[15]

If Bergman had little advice for those who ventured on spiritual journeys, it was because he knew that these belonged to the unknown and unpredictable. Each man experiences his journey alone, and each finds the spiritual guides that make his path possible and fruitful. In looking back on his life, Bergman was convinced that his experience in Prague had taught him much. He remembered something that Kafka had written at the age of thirteen in his album: "There is a coming and a going, a separating but often no reuniting." He reflected on these words and wondered if Kafka knew the meaning they unveiled. Now at ninety-one, Bergman remarked that it seemed to him that "we can interpret these words as a warning for generations. They awaken us to the divisions of mankind which are necessary but only as divisions within a unity in which there is a reuniting. The final goal of mankind can be only a greater and stronger union. We are children of the One God."[16]

Bergman's experience of Prague was unique. Middle Europe had always been prey to either the ambitions of Russia or Germany. Small countries learn how to avoid that hunger of the large ones; they learn the value of cooperation and a profound distaste for war. They fight for independence physically and spiritually, and they need protection to survive. They know how easily they can be absorbed and struggle to

---
[15]*Ibid.*, 5/6/73.
[16]*Ibid.*, 1/22/74.

create their own cultural heritage as a protection against this absorption. They ask earnestly if they want to be the people of Huss or *The Good Soldier Schweik.* For small nations like Czechoslovakia these cultural questions are vital. They are deeply sensitive to their literary contributions, and peace is necessary for their survival. They are the greatest Kantians.

Bergman's remarks on division are significant; they reflect his final considerations. "Division," he said, "is always a view on the coming reunion. If I think back to the work of my own generation of *Bar Kochba,* (in Prague), of Theodor Herzl, and it seems to me that this uniting of opposites was characteristic of what Jews did at this time: men like Robert Weltsch and Hans Kohn, Leo and Hugo Herrmann. We took Prague to our heart like as a *Brueckenstadt* (a bridge) and sought to carry out the uniting of opposites. It is probably no accident that the Bohemian Jews were the bearers of the idea of *Brit Shalom.* This is the teaching which we hand over to our successors."[17]

Bergman never failed to see problems, and where he sought resolution, he found disharmony; but never are these depths of pessimism the realizations of the failure of philosophy and the despair of faith. Bergman was deeply influenced by the unfinished quality of the universe. The future contained the promise and hope of the idea of mankind. From the future we construct the history of mankind. Without this hope and revelation, man sinks into cultural despair, war and disorder. If we listen to the words of England's great twentieth century philosopher R.G. Collingwood, we hear words which live on the dark side of Bergman's faith. "Whenever a school of philosophy is sick of a mortal illness," Collingwood observed, "this symptom never fails to appear. I mean pessimism. Pessimism is the reaction of the human intellect to a hopelessly false philosophy. Struggling to understand the world in terms of the false philosophy which it has learned to believe, and finding it impossible, the mind is driven to despair; and pessimism is another word for despair. In the person of Schopenhauer and Edouard Von Hartmann, the German mind showed, to anyone who could understand, that it was suffering from a deadly disease; and Schopenhauer himself was conscious that the disease was the philosophy of Hegel. It is the spiritual disease that has caused the war (W.W.I.)."[18]

If pessimism had not become a serious disease, then it is to the honor of the philosophers that the illness was kept away. But the philosophers die, politics change and there is no predictability that allows us to believe

---

[17]*Ibid.*
[18]"The Prussian Philosophy," (1919) in *Essays in Political Philosophy* (Oxford, Clarendon Press, 1989), 203.

that pessimism will not infect the community of mankind unless philosophers speak of hope and ideals. Collingwood had spoken of "the absolute theory of the State, which drives every state that holds it into a career of aggression, and conquest, and tyranny – a career like that of a mad dog, only to be quieted in death – the theory was the root of the war from which we are now emerging, and it is only the eradication of this theory that can give us peace."[19]

Bergman feared the consequences of despotic nationalism and it was this danger which he faced desperately in the last years of his life. The spiritual dimension of life seems to fade into the secular and the universal prophetic visions become absorbed in the games of daily politics. We know that human society has rarely been otherwise, but the philosopher's responsibility remains the Idea and faith in his future.

Bergman's last diary entry was a letter to his son and daughter-in-law Schlomo and Ridi. Nothing could give him greater pleasure than to tell them that the fourth volume of his *History of Philosophy* had been completed. He told them that he had sent the publisher essays on Hegel, Maimon, Brentano, Bolzano, Herbart, Cohen, Schopenhauer, Edouard Von Hartmann, and Max Adler. The third volume was dedicated to Schelling. Bergman then stated: "I write this letter to New York not knowing whether you are there or on the way to India. I urge you ardently to visit Pondicherry and the Ashram of Sri Aurobindo."[20]

Work was a holy activity for Bergman and the love of old spiritual companions like Sri Aurobindo remained until the end. Like every great philosopher, his life was the creation of a world of values and personalities.

In the tranquility of his attitude and the tolerance of his spirit, we rarely encountered Bergman's opposition to the ideas of those around him, and even more unique are those incidents that show his criticism of those close to him. In his article on Buber, contributed to the Buber volume of *The Library of Living Philosophers*, Bergman spoke of two vital issues that separated him from Buber: the upper world and the Messiah. Bergman noted that in one of Buber's essays in the *Origin and Meaning of Hasidism*, he asked, "What concern of ours, if they exist, are the upper worlds?" Bergman replied, "This appears to me to be an inadmissible simplification. For if there were upper worlds and man could know them, that would be tantamount to the more tremendous revolution. But even if they should turn out to be nothing more than projections of your subjectivity, they would have taught us decisive things concerning man. With respect to these upper worlds, we have the same *obligation* as in

---

[19]*Ibid.*
[20]*Tagebuecher & Briefe*, 2/6/75.

regard to the world present to our senses."[21] The direction of Bergman's thought was uniquely and finely distinguished from his colleagues' in Jerusalem. In his search for the "upper worlds," Bergman found a level of communication with world thinkers that was ecumenical in the deepest sense. In this communication, Bergman's thought was radically new.

In reference to Buber's remark that "it is a mistake to regard Jewish Messianism as exhausted by a belief in an event happening once at the end of time and in a single human figure created at the center of this event.... The Messiahship at the end of time is preceded by one of all times poured out over the ages." Bergman found himself troubled by this formulation because he found in it the suppression of actuality of the Messianic age. Buber's thought, he said, "suppresses, I am afraid, any real belief in the ultimate Messiahship – in the redemption of nature, in the overcoming of hostile forces and the conquest of death. I understand Buber's reluctance, possibly in order to clarify his departure from his own youthful position or to set himself apart from the enthusiasts who 'seek to accelerate the end,' to speak of the All-Day of redemption'.... But it is my belief that in spite of all such hazards, it is our obligation precisely, at this time to hold fast to the reality and concreteness of the ultimate goal of redemption, to strengthen the awareness of such concreteness, and to measure the progress off many by this goal. Otherwise there is the danger that in our efforts to serve reason and to remain true to the earth, we shall forget the meaning of human existence."[22] In the calmness of these words, lay a radical distinction between Buber and Bergman. The latter's belief in the concreteness of the Messiah and his rejection of any attempt to reduce it to the dimensions of reason, show clearly the depths of Bergman's religious commitment. This faith was primarily rooted in the tradition and only secondarily in the dictates of reason or in the poetical imagination.

In his last words of Buber, Bergman stated that "it appears to me that at this point his (Buber's) thought remains enmeshed in a rationalistic prejudice and that he is readily paying tribute to the world view of the nineteenth century. It is necessary to pierce through these limitations if we are to develop further Buber's own thought in the direction of that 'Great Reality' of which the mystical books of his youth gave evidence, and to which Buber's life work shows us the way."[23] What we truly find in these words, is a description of the way Bergman traveled beyond

---

[21]"Martin Buber and Mysticism" in *The Philosophy of Martin Buber*, ed. P.A. Schlipp (LaSalle, Illinois, Open Court, 1967), 308.
[22]*Ibid.*, 305-306.
[23]*Ibid.*, 308.

Buber. Through Buber, he projected the new directions of his thinking. This was a path Bergman often followed. The reader must be able to see that the insights he ascribed to others became the power of his own thought and faith.

Bergman could leave no disciples. He showed those close to him the ways but never "the way." For those who seek in him a system there is constant disappointment; for those who have the courage and faith to journey alone, there is much that Bergman teaches. The fact that no religious faith is absolute, allows every great tradition to reveal itself to others, to be explored fully, and for men to realize that God's spirit has multiple forms. Each man must live from a tradition, but there are no barriers that we cannot overcome in our search to comprehend how others journey towards God. Bergman's thought and personality is a way rather than a doctrine. At times we ask why he didn't explore this or that faith more deeply. I often wondered why he failed to comprehend the Platonic structure of Roman Catholicism, and why he and Buber found greater congeniality with Protestant thinkers. We wonder why this great ideal community did not have much influence on either Buber or Bergman.

When we think of the *Ecclesia Mater* and we hear the words of that great Catholic theologian Henri Cardinal de Lebac, that "in Her (the Church's) very visibility, the Church is the vital nucleus around which gather from age to age, and in ways often hidden from us, all those who are to be saved. Those whom she has already united are truly the soul of the world, the soul of this great human body."[24]

Bergman's ecumenism made it possible for each of us to be open to the Spirit in all directions. There are no conclusions, and no summaries are possible; there are only new journeys and new experiences made in the Light of the Spirit. Each seeker is a member of an unseen community of men and women who have through the ages sought to find the reality of man, the worlds of consciousness that are yet to be explored, and the "divine food" that has come from the heavens, but has yet to be known by man. Bergman had a deep feeling for community; he lived for the ideal of a believing community devoted to the oneness of God.

If, in conclusion, I cite the words of Augustine, recalled for us by Cardinal de Lubac in 1941 in a lecture at Lyon, warning of the damages of anti-Semitism, I am sure they would be happily approved by Bergman as expressing his hopes. If Augustine addressed these words to the Church, Bergman would address them to the same spiritual community encompassing all faiths. Augustine's words are: "By a bond not only of common life but of true brotherhood, you unite citizens to citizens, races

---

[24]The Splendors of the Church (London, Sheed and Ward, 1979), 177.

to races, in a word, all men to each other, by reminding them of their common origin (De Moribus Ecclesiae Catholicae)"[25] It is odd to think that a life's work finds only a few words which bring together its hopes and activities, but they do, and we must listen carefully to them.

---

[25]*Catholic Resistance to Anti-Semitism* (San Francisco, Ignatius Press, 1990), 25.

Inconclusive Conclusions

Hugo Bergman learned the philosophical and theological way through a power and a gift: the gift of faith and the power of listening. With this gift, he sought to struggle against every force that violated and made mockery of justice and goodness. With his listening, he absorbed the spiritual ways of man from all parts of the world. He heard the words they used and created to find their goals and purposes in a world that needed their hopes and faiths. Bergman knew that no believer could or wanted to escape his tradition and way of life, but the believer did not demand its superiority or its exclusivity. Bergman's Jewishness became the source of his universalism. He drew from it a message for mankind. In this message, he was prepared to hear the messages of others, not only to comprehend them intellectually, but to hear the spirit of God in them. He listened to them intensively. He did not only hear the words of other faiths, he heard the men who spoke them. He had learned from Rudolf Steiner that there were higher levels of consciousness. The spirit of God gave him the possibilities of intuitive understanding and the depths of imagination. Man was incomplete, and his spiritual destiny had only begun to be revealed to him.

Bergman's thought defies conclusions. His philosophy will grow as one man after another returns to it for the inspiration that comes from the philosopher whose thinking cannot be imitated, but only experienced and imagined. From Bergman, we learn to approach philosophy and begin our journey toward it. Bergman hovers over us like a shadow in whose cover we walk and think. We read other thinkers and imagine what Bergman would have said, how deeply he would have appreciated their remarks, and how powerfully he would have felt the impact of the spirit in them. I realized this in a study of the Jesuit fathers who fought the anti-Semitism of both the Germans and Pétainistes from 1940 to 1944 in Lyon.

Henri Cardinal de Lubac in his study of *Christian Resistance to Anti-Semitism: Memories from 1940-1944* (1988), gives us a monumental view and a sensitive insight into the activities of a group of Jesuit fathers. "While Fr. Fessard," he wrote, "was writing his *France, Prends garde*...in Lyon, and Fr. Chaillet from the hill of Fourvière, was continuing the clandestine preparations that were to end in the launching of his Cahiers, Fr. Yves de Montcheuil, their confrere and friend, could not participate in the enterprise, for demobilization had led him directly to Paris, the *Études* house directed by Fr. d'Ouince from which he wrote me on July 3, 1940, "So here I am, safe and sound, but as you can imagine very sad, with no illusions about the 'honorable' facade of an aged and circumvented Pétain."[1]

Bergman listened carefully to those who fought for the spiritual values of civilization, to those who fought to enlighten mankind to the distortions which the maliciousness of modern paganism brought to human life. He knew that the struggle against idolatry was a burden on every faith, and when faiths fought faiths, they weakened their forces against their common enemy: myth and mythologies.

What were the words that Father Yves de Montcheuil told youth groups in 1941? Father de Lubac gives us a few quotations: "In its overall tonality, German racism...is profoundly foreign to us. The pantheism of race, this rooting of man in nature, this important given to 'blood' and 'soul' are difficult for us to absorb. Yet it is difficult to believe that it is going to remain without any influence on us.... The whole Christian spirit is being attacked by this *en bloc*. It is not only religious practice or belonging to the Church that is disappearing, but people are seeking a scale of opposite values. Now what is essentially necessary is to reject the criterion adopted for judging Christianity. The primary goal for Christianity is not temporal success, but the spiritual transformation of man.... Nazism has obtained its success only by ruining man.... There is no time for flirting with it or being hesitant about it. It must be clearly shown that the grandeur it gives is not pure, and the moral monstrosities that it not only tolerates but provokes must be emphasized."[2]

Bergman was convinced that we are all bearers of the moral and spiritual struggle against idolatry. If he would have known these Jesuit fathers and all the others who worked with them, he would have shared their devotion and hopes, he would have followed their work with love and fidelity. He felt a fraternal bond with men who knew that life which emerged from the love of God was in every way a battle for a God, who depended upon our assistance for His realization in His creation. This assistanceship bears that suffering that greets us with indifference and

---
[1] *Catholic Resistance to Anti-Semitism*, 215.
[2] *Ibid.*, 256.

rejection. Bergman would always think of a poem that gave him courage and succor:

> I sought God and I have not found Him
> I pursue Him and I cannot reach Him
> I have drawn Him into my system
> But my thinking was too small for Him
> God has delivered me from my searchings
> I never searched alone
> *He* sought me and found me
> Now I am His and He is finally mine.[3]

The work of the spirit is always a companionship, I am with Him and He is with me. The man of faith knows that he is never alone, that his courage is not his, and that his faith is a gift. His fidelity is his hope and truthfulness.

Bergman would have been deeply moved by the confession of faith that Yves de Montcheuil wrote in March 1944, five months before his death. The text was called, "The Spiritual Bases of Our Commitment." It begins with these words, "It is not to a human cause that we are making the gift of our person, to which we are consecrating ourselves without reserve, but to the Kingdom of God, to the continuation consequently of the work of Christ. This spiritual enterprise must, then, have spiritual, not human, bases.... Without doubt, all those who put something too human into their commitment, will not end in such catastrophes, and that human part can be very variable besides. But in the very measure in which the motives of our commitment are not supernatural, it will be ineffective. This is one of the fundamental lessons of the Gospel: the Kingdom of God is found only by those who live by the spirit of the Kingdom of God, who seek it for itself."[4]

How deeply sympathetic Bergman would have been to these words, can be clearly seen from the fact that he never sought to define types of faith, never sought to see radical distinctions and proclaim the truthfulness of one over the other. Bergman went beyond these conflicts of definitions, he longed for a community of faith that surpassed doctrinal differences. He passed beyond distinctions to that faithful commitment that Father de Montcheuil spoke of as the way of man. Bergman visioned Zionism as the sanctification of the Holy Name. He understood well the Kingdom of God as the command and obligation confronting life. It was not only what a man said but the realization of his words that impressed Bergman. The work of the Jesuit fathers would have deeply affected him, their devotion to Israel as the source of their

---

[3]*Tagebuecher & Briefe*, 11/27/64.
[4]*Catholic Resistance to Anti-Semitism*, 224-225.

Christian faith would have confirmed his belief in that unseen community of the faithful whose strength and hope came forth from the presence of the Kingdom.

Father de Montcheuil remarked that, left to oneself, "we would have taken different routes according to our character, our inclinations, and circumstances; we would never have taken that one, we would never have loved the Kingdom of God for itself. And much more: *we are only following an inclination, an impulse given to us by grace.* Our Lord not only shows us the road; he gets us to walk it. Our progress is always only an acceptance and, as it were, an abandonment to the impulse that he communicates to us. All that we give him comes in reality from him."[5] These words of faith go beyond the I-Thou relationship which in its essence remains secular and rational. They embody the mystery of divine love and man's hesitant responses. In this mystery, Bergman found more than a relationship. He found the encompassing power of God's majesty and the awe that it arouses in us. This is an awe that gives us no rest; it drives us to renewed activity and to a never-ending work.

We realize the essence of man to be in divine dependence and partnership. Father de Montcheuil stated it well, "He can overcome all external obstacles and change hearts without any assistance. *If then, he calls us, it is through love for us; he wants to give us this grandeur and this dignity of being his assistants.... If we walk in generosity, our Lord will ask much of us.*"[6] Every faith has its formulations and ways of expression, but behind them lives their divine trust and commitment. The sensitivity to these revealed Bergman's extraordinary powers. He went beyond disputes and oppositions. He never sought superiority or grandeur for one faith in terms of the other. Each was a path created in tradition, in the Magisterium that set its course, its direction and goal. From the love of his tradition, from the spiritual Zionism to which he had given his life, there arose this rare and unique quality to hear the voices that live in the faith of others. His was a philosophy of "sympathy," of a culture consciousness that embraced in love all those ways that were in search of the uniqueness of God's oneness.

Often we ask about the burdens the Lord places upon us. We hear the prophet Micah proclaim, "What does He demand of us?" We know the weight of his love and we ask only for the strength to do our work in His service. Father de Montcheuil reminded us that "the latter (human leaders) can ask heavy things, but they have only a weak, and at times very limited, part in making others capable of doing these things. Our Lord is for us, he who asks and he who gives us the strength to

---

[5]*Ibid.*, 125.
[6]*Ibid.*, 226.

accomplish. So we can be assured that there will never be a conflict between the two, if we pray as we should. We can live then in serenity. Let us repeat with St. Augustine, "Lord, give what you command, and command what you wish."[7]

This ultimate trust in God was, for Bergman, the beginning for all that he did and thought. In and from this trust in life, he received the strength and force which enabled him to hear philosophy, to be active in politics, to create an ideal for a new state of Israel. Again and again, he never ventured into the realm of the absolute to find exclusivity and *a* truth to set aside all truths. He knew that man's consciousness and conscience were developing and that from different perspectives and traditions, men had fought for divine enlightenment, they had battled against idolatry, and struggled against the suffocation of arbitrary formulations. In this world truth belongs only to God and men wonder about its embracing powers, but know that no one captures its majesty. We each struggle with our traditions and experiences to approach the divine. Father de Montcheuil could speak of the living "tradition of the Church." He thought of it as "an inexhaustible spring that, as it flows forth, to use the words of Saint Irenaeus, never ceases to bring forth life to the vase that receives it.... Great causes," he stated, "are strong in the sacrifices they demand and not in the concessions they make for the mediocre in order to hold them."[8]

This inexhaustible spring was for Bergman the idea, the eternal form of Israel. It gave him life and his fidelity was the source of his creativity, of his faith and hope. He lived from the idea, he comprehended how man lived from the Church, and how others like Sri Aurobindo, Rudolf Steiner, Frithjof Schuon, Hermann Cohen, Leonhard Ragaz, could live from their fidelity to God's presence. In the presence of God, there is no anti-Semitism as there is no rejection of faith by faith. Bergman wrote again and again about ecumenism. He believed that it was the way of the future.

Bergman believed that events in history were trials that tested man's moral integrity. God was always present, although His presence defied and overpowered our understanding. We wait in patience and fidelity for the meanings that flow from His being with us. In the Eichmann decision, Bergman believed that "history had given Judaism and the State of Israel an unbelievable chance to show the world that it is ready to end the dance of death, the dance of murder and revenge. It was a

---

[7]*Ibid.*
[8]*Ibid.*, 228.

great chance for us and for the world. We could have shown the world that we are not a state like other states. We rejected this chance."[9]

Bergman knew well that events test men's beliefs. He would have deeply felt the struggles of the Fathers in Lyon. The words of Father de Montcheuil, of Fathers Fessard, and Chaillet, of Henri Cardinal de Lubac, would have been precious for him. Against the idolatries of racism, statism, and ideological secularism was the word of God, the living word that drew men toward the presence of the Kingdom and gave them the challenge which it demanded of them. In the context of the politics in both Palestine and Israel, Bergman and his companions fought the unending battle for love, compassion and justice, the battle which God had given to them, and to all men, from eternity.

We have inconclusive conclusions. In the realm of the spirit there is only the struggles of love and fidelity. The presence of God, even in his absence, is the reality that explains all realities; explanations remain tentative and profoundly inadequate. In every faith the same courage and truthfulness tests the human soul. We know only simple things; we know that the divine spirit in us is the creative source of our being; it is always more than we can grasp, but in that more that is always beyond our logic, lives the power of our lives. This we share with all men. "We are spiritually Semites" and in this spirit we all find our faith. Bergman, like the Jesuit fathers, knew this well.

Bergman's article "The Need for a Courageous Philosophy" is the closest he ever came to a personal statement about his philosophical faith. The question that constantly dominated his thought was: How can man respond to the "higher worlds" that determine and nourish his existence and its history? In reply, he said, "Perhaps man has to put up with this horizontal, causal, mechanistic interpretation only because he *cannot* raise himself above the mechanical world revealed to him by the senses."[10] Bergman refused such a resignation to the senses and the concepts of the understanding. he believed that there were means to the "higher worlds" and man had to discover them. "Such means do exist," he exclaimed. "Philosophical schools such as the Pythagoreans and the Neo-Platonists taught how to rise and progress, and in India any past theoretical philosopher is at the same time a great practical yogi. This is actually the task of philosophy, art and religion, to show man the way to that height of which we have spoken."[11]

Philosophy needs again to assume her role as Queen of the Arts and Sciences. She must guide man to the higher levels of consciousness, to

---

[9]*Briefe & Tagebuecher*, 6/1/62.
[10]"The Need for a Courageous Philosophy."
[11]*Ibid.*, 118.

relationships that are not only understood, but become the means to higher realms of reality. "Therefore," Bergman remarked, "the philosopher has to see and understand that immediate consciousness is only a small sector of a whole range of possible awareness.... The philosopher must strive, as far as he is able, to expand his consciousness. He should regard all examples of a broader experience, which may be presented to him, not only with critical intelligence, but also with a readiness to believe, with a feeling of awe for a truth given to others and not to him. He has to listen, absorb, receive, and learn with reverence.... Wide and limitless horizons will open up to philosophy as soon as it dares to be truly philosophy, which is the love of wisdom."[12] The philosopher must again assert his love of wisdom.

No further words are needed to show the path that Bergman traveled. His was a lover of wisdom, a love that led him to become aware of higher worlds of reality. He sought not only the truths that came from the world around him, but the truth that came from above, the Logos, the Light, that allow our eyes to see spiritually. Bergman was a Pythagorean listener. He knew that a spiritual listening and seeing brought man from the world of the senses to the contemplation of truth and beauty. What most men learned to cast aside as a metaphysical wasteland became for Bergman ways to God.

---

[12]*Ibid.*, 119.

Index

Abraham, 3, 24, 50, 58, 92, 129, 137
Adler, Max, 55, 145
Alain, 126
Amalek, 17
Angel, 8, 77, 92, 107
Anthropomorphism, 119
Anthroposophic, 41, 141
Arab, 24, 82, 109-110, 139, 142
Aristotle, 14, 32, 39
Ashram, 17, 31, 77, 83, 138-139, 145
Atheism, 98
Athens, 126
Augustine, 3, 85, 87, 90-93, 143, 147, 153
Aurobindo, Sri, 3, 16-17, 19, 31, 52, 56, 66-67, 76-77, 83, 87, 104, 137-139, 145, 153
Auschwitz, 47
Bar Kochba, 139, 144
Barakhot, 19
Barth, Karl, 49, 54, 92
Bergman, Shmuel Hugo, 1-5, 11-20, 21-33, 35-47, 49-64, 65-67, 69-77, 79-80, 81-93, 95-105, 107-113, 115-124, 125-134, 135-147, 149-155
Bergson, Henri, 76
Bhagavadgita, 19
Blanchot, Maurice, 22
Blumenfeld, Kurt, 108
Bokser, Ben Zion, 66
Bolzano, Bernhard, 1, 110, 145
Brentano, Franz, 1, 99, 110, 145
Brod, Max, 100
Brueckendasein, 100
Brunner, Ferdinand, 29
Buber, Martin, 1, 11, 19-20, 43, 49, 51-52, 55, 58, 76, 82-83, 97-98, 110-111, 126, 138, 145-147
Buddhism, 1, 86
Cain, 130
Camus, 129
Carmelite, 5
Cassandra, 1
Cassirer, Ernst, 1-3, 116-117, 123-124
Cassirer, Toni, 117, 124
Catholicism, 56, 135, 140, 147-148, 150-151

Chaillet, Père Pierre, 150, 154
Christ, 56-57, 90, 126, 151
Christianity, 1, 16, 19, 26, 30, 52-53, 55-56, 58-62, 64, 66, 68, 76-77, 79, 81, 86, 90, 92, 118, 125, 127, 131, 149-150, 152
Christocentric, 79
Christus, 49
Civilization, 4, 12, 57, 117-120, 150
Clericalism, 60
Cohen, Hermann, 1, 7-11, 15-17, 19, 42, 50-51, 55, 60, 83, 85, 92-93, 145, 153
Collingwood, R.G., 144-145
Cosmogenesis, 78
Covenant, 3, 10-11, 15-17, 56-57, 62, 92
Creator, 37, 44, 46, 51, 63, 69, 88, 120, 122
Czechoslovakia, 82, 144
Daniel, 67
Darwin, Charles, 69
Deification, 17, 54, 56, 59
Democritus, 10
Determinism, 112
Deuteronomy, 92
Devekuth, 63
Diotima, 14, 142
Eckhart, Meister, 29
Ecumenism, 20, 55, 57, 60, 62, 67, 133, 147, 153
Edom, 17
Eichmann, 153
Einstein, Albert, 107-113
Eisner, Kurt, 55

Eucharist, 66, 75
Eudaemonism, 18
Fanta, Bertha, 104, 108
Fessard, Gaston, 150, 154
Fichte, J.G., 1, 3, 19, 67
Fleischmann, Jacob, 81, 84-87
Flusser, David, 91, 131
Freud, Sigmund, 31
Gentile, 17
Germany, 50, 73, 76, 82, 97, 100, 107-109, 125, 143-144, 149-150
Ghetto-Angst, 131
Gnosticism, 128-129
Gods, 10, 13, 19, 28, 39, 54, 59, 92
Goethe, 41-45
Gospel, 151
Goy, 17
Greek, 82, 115, 126
Guardini, Romano, 19, 87, 140
Guénon, René, 52, 87
Hapsburg Empire, 108
Hartmann, Edouard von, 110, 144-145
Hasidism, 145
Hebraism, 125
Hebrew, 58, 73, 91, 109, 125, 129, 131, 137
Hegel, Georg W.F., 81, 84-85, 92, 108, 138, 144-145
Heidegger, Martin, 44, 72
Hermann, Luise, 127
Herrmann, Hugo, 144
Herrmann, Leo, 144

Index

Herzl, Theodor, 77, 144
Hinduism, 1, 86
Histadrut, 109
Hoelderlin, 92
Holiness, 62, 66, 70, 72, 122
Holy Temple, 90
Humanism, 3, 5, 11, 15-17, 20, 55, 58, 120, 125, 139
Humanitarianism, 120
Hume, David, 40
Huss, John, 144
Idolatry, 8, 17, 54, 59, 62, 130, 132-133, 150, 153
Idols, 8, 92
Immorality, 24
Immortality, 13-15, 17, 32, 36, 38, 45, 72, 79, 136, 140
Incarnation, 27, 66, 75, 93, 103, 127, 137
India, 3, 16-17, 31, 52, 76-77, 83, 91, 137, 139, 145, 154
Isaac, 3, 65-66, 68, 71-72
Isaiah, 71, 89, 128
Islam, 86
James, William, 138
Japan, 109
Jaspers, Karl, 21-26, 30, 33
Jerusalem, 1, 4-5, 11, 21, 47, 57, 63, 73, 76, 82, 87, 99, 104, 109, 126, 140, 146
Jesuit, 26, 65, 113, 149-151, 154
Jesus, 57, 60, 62, 86, 89-91, 125-126, 131
Job, 58, 130
Judaism, 1, 4, 7, 17-19, 24, 30-31, 50-51, 53-62, 64, 66-67, 76-77, 82, 84, 86, 90-93, 98, 100, 107-108, 125-126, 128, 130, 133, 149, 153
Jung, Carl, 40
Kabbalah, 29
Kafka, Franz, 29, 53, 95-104, 107, 115-116, 139, 142-143
Kant, Immanuel, 1, 9, 15, 24, 37-40, 42, 44-46, 70, 76, 82-84, 110, 116, 121-122, 131, 142-143
Kantian, 93, 135, 144
Karma, 137
Kierkegaard, Sören, 15
Kohn, Hans, 1, 144
Kook, Abraham Isaac, 52, 56, 65-75, 77, 104
Landauer, Gustav, 55
Laurentius, Bruder, 91
Leibnitz, 1
London, 39, 59, 98, 108, 127, 147
Lubac, Henri de, 27, 147, 149-150, 154
Mach, Ernst, 107
Maimon, Solomon, 19, 145
Marburg, 8
Marty, Anton, 1, 107, 110
Marx, Karl, 49
Masaryk, Thomas, 82
Materialism, 22, 26, 42, 66
Messiah, 7-8, 45, 51, 55-56, 62-63, 145-146
Messiahship, 146
Messianism, 7, 9-10, 12, 51, 55, 76, 90, 92-93, 146
Metaphysics, 3, 5, 12, 15, 27, 32, 36, 39-40, 85, 95, 137, 155

Micah, 60, 152
Monotheism, 8, 10-11, 13, 15, 18, 85, 90-91, 93
Moralists, 74
Moses, 24, 63, 86, 92
Muslim, 52
Mysticism, 29, 69, 91, 140, 146
Myth, 8-10, 36, 41, 90, 117, 123-124, 128, 131-132, 150
Mythology, 8-10, 150
Nationalism, 7, 49, 51, 55, 82, 100, 110, 116, 139, 145
New Testament, 91, 131
Newton, Isaac, 108-109
Nicholus of Cusa, 1
Nihilism, 22, 26, 95
Orthodoxy, 84, 104
Ouspensky, F.D., 18, 132
Pacificism, 55
Paganism, 18, 21, 150
Palestine, 1, 49-51, 58, 70, 75, 83, 98-99, 109, 154
Pantheism, 75, 98, 104, 150
Parable, 81, 91, 95, 104, 142
Parapsychology, 108
Pascal, Blaise, 87
Paul, 60, 90, 92-93
Peace, 3, 78, 109, 121, 142, 144-145
Petrément, Simone, 125, 127, 129-132
Phaedo, 28-29, 32
Picht, Georg, 19, 87, 113
Platonists, 31, 154
Pondicherry, 31, 77, 138-139, 145

Prometheus, 8
Prophet, 18, 51, 54, 56, 58, 60, 62-63, 66, 83, 89-90, 92-93, 141, 152
Protestantism, 53, 56, 135, 147
Psalmist, 61
Pythagoras, 15, 28
Pythagorean, 31, 49, 86, 154-155
Racism, 150, 154
Radl, Emmanuel, 30
Ragaz, Leonhard, 19, 49-50, 52-59, 61-64, 153
Ramakrishna, 91
Realism, 12, 51, 109-110
Reincarnation, 137
Rilke, R.M., 107
Rosenheim, Jacob, 119
Rosenzweig, Franz, 1, 60, 83, 132
Rotenstreich, Nathan, 1, 82, 142
Sacredness, 15, 79-80, 93, 103, 109, 118-120, 122
Sacrifice, 19, 39, 63, 91, 98, 127, 129, 139, 153
Salvation, 8, 32, 53, 89, 126, 129
Sanctification, 12, 17, 19, 41, 51, 55, 57, 75, 79, 139, 151
Santa Theresa, 132
Scheler, Max, 2
Schelling, F.W., 1, 5, 19, 42, 145
Schocken, Salmon S., 7, 50, 58, 69, 101, 125

Scholem, Gershom, 1, 7, 19-20, 52, 82, 138
Schopenhauer, Arthur, 144-145
Schuon, Frithjof, 3, 52, 87, 140, 153
Schweitzer, Albert, 115-120, 122-124
Secularism, 56, 154
Sefirah, 29
Sefirot, 29
Simon, Ernst, 1, 52, 82
Sinai, 70
Socialism, 49-50, 53, 55, 68, 95, 104
Socrates, 29, 35-36, 123
Sophist, 8, 12, 24
Spinoza, 138
Spirituality, 22, 137-138
Steiner, Rudolf, 18, 36, 41-43, 45-47, 76, 87, 108, 132, 141-142, 149, 153
Stiehm, Lothar, 115
Strasbourg, 125
Stumpf, Carl, 99
Sufi, 3, 140
Sulzberger, Jean, 135-136
Supernatural, 75, 151
Surrealism, 70
Sweden, 116
Switzerland, 49-50, 53
Talmud, 8, 19, 86, 121
Taubes, Jacob, 92
Teilhard de Chardin, Pierre, 65-66, 73, 104, 113

Tel Aviv, 109
Tertullian, 47
Teshuvah, 70-72
Theodicy, 18
Theology, 49, 68, 78, 90, 92
Theomorphism, 119
Theosophy, 41, 104
Tolstoy, 22
Torah, 8
Totalitarianism, 51, 59, 72
Trinity, 62, 126
Universalism, 17, 51, 65, 79, 82, 89, 91, 100, 109, 125, 149
Uppsala, 116-117
Ursprung, 10
Urvaeter, 103
Ussishkin, Menachem, 109
Utilitarianism, 22
Utopia, 113
Weil, Simone, 125-131, 133
Weltsch, Felix, 1, 52-53, 100, 130, 138
Weltsch, Robert, 1, 52, 113, 138, 144
Wust, Peter, 19
Yves de Montcheuil, 26-27, 150-154
Zechariah, 11, 83
Zeus, 8
Zion, 49, 51, 66, 87, 97-98
Zionism, 3, 51, 53, 58, 75, 86, 90, 95-99, 104, 108, 139, 151-152
Zionist, 4, 51, 63, 95-98, 108

Brown Judaic Studies

140001	*Approaches to Ancient Judaism I*	William S. Green
140002	*The Traditions of Eleazar Ben Azariah*	Tzvee Zahavy
140003	*Persons and Institutions in Early Rabbinic Judaism*	William S. Green
140004	*Claude Goldsmid Montefiore on the Ancient Rabbis*	Joshua B. Stein
140005	*The Ecumenical Perspective and the Modernization of Jewish Religion*	S. Daniel Breslauer
140006	*The Sabbath-Law of Rabbi Meir*	Robert Goldenberg
140007	*Rabbi Tarfon*	Joel Gereboff
140008	*Rabban Gamaliel II*	Shamai Kanter
140009	*Approaches to Ancient Judaism II*	William S. Green
140010	*Method and Meaning in Ancient Judaism*	Jacob Neusner
140011	*Approaches to Ancient Judaism III*	William S. Green
140012	*Turning Point: Zionism and Reform Judaism*	Howard R. Greenstein
140013	*Buber on God and the Perfect Man*	Pamela Vermes
140014	*Scholastic Rabbinism*	Anthony J. Saldarini
140015	*Method and Meaning in Ancient Judaism II*	Jacob Neusner
140016	*Method and Meaning in Ancient Judaism III*	Jacob Neusner
140017	*Post Mishnaic Judaism in Transition*	Baruch M. Bokser
140018	*A History of the Mishnaic Law of Agriculture: Tractate Maaser Sheni*	Peter J. Haas
140019	*Mishnah's Theology of Tithing*	Martin S. Jaffee
140020	*The Priestly Gift in Mishnah: A Study of Tractate Terumot*	Alan. J. Peck
140021	*History of Judaism: The Next Ten Years*	Baruch M. Bokser
140022	*Ancient Synagogues*	Joseph Gutmann
140023	*Warrant for Genocide*	Norman Cohn
140024	*The Creation of the World According to Gersonides*	Jacob J. Staub
140025	*Two Treatises of Philo of Alexandria: A Commentary on De Gigantibus and Quod Deus Sit Immutabilis*	Winston/Dillon
140026	*A History of the Mishnaic Law of Agriculture: Kilayim*	Irving Mandelbaum
140027	*Approaches to Ancient Judaism IV*	William S. Green
140028	*Judaism in the American Humanities*	Jacob Neusner
140029	*Handbook of Synagogue Architecture*	Marilyn Chiat
140030	*The Book of Mirrors*	Daniel C. Matt
140031	*Ideas in Fiction: The Works of Hayim Hazaz*	Warren Bargad
140032	*Approaches to Ancient Judaism V*	William S. Green
140033	*Sectarian Law in the Dead Sea Scrolls: Courts, Testimony and the Penal Code*	Lawrence H. Schiffman
140034	*A History of the United Jewish Appeal: 1939-1982*	Marc L. Raphael
140035	*The Academic Study of Judaism*	Jacob Neusner
140036	*Woman Leaders in the Ancient Synagogue*	Bernadette Brooten
140037	*Formative Judaism: Religious, Historical, and Literary Studies*	Jacob Neusner
140038	*Ben Sira's View of Women: A Literary Analysis*	Warren C. Trenchard
140039	*Barukh Kurzweil and Modern Hebrew Literature*	James S. Diamond
140040	*Israeli Childhood Stories of the Sixties: Yizhar, Aloni, Shahar, Kahana-Carmon*	Gideon Telpaz
140041	*Formative Judaism II: Religious, Historical, and Literary Studies*	Jacob Neusner
140042	*Judaism in the American Humanities II: Jewish Learning and the New Humanities*	Jacob Neusner

140043	Support for the Poor in the Mishnaic Law of Agriculture: Tractate Peah	Roger Brooks
140044	The Sanctity of the Seventh Year: A Study of Mishnah Tractate Shebiit	Louis E. Newman
140045	Character and Context: Studies in the Fiction of Abramovitsh, Brenner, and Agnon	Jeffrey Fleck
140046	Formative Judaism III: Religious, Historical, and Literary Studies	Jacob Neusner
140047	Pharaoh's Counsellors: Job, Jethro, and Balaam in Rabbinic and Patristic Tradition	Judith Baskin
140048	The Scrolls and Christian Origins: Studies in the Jewish Background of the New Testament	Matthew Black
140049	Approaches to Modern Judaism I	Marc Lee Raphael
140050	Mysterious Encounters at Mamre and Jabbok	William T. Miller
140051	The Mishnah Before 70	Jacob Neusner
140052	Sparda by the Bitter Sea: Imperial Interaction in Western Anatolia	Jack Martin Balcer
140053	Hermann Cohen: The Challenge of a Religion of Reason	William Kluback
140054	Approaches to Judaism in Medieval Times I	David R. Blumenthal
140055	In the Margins of the Yerushalmi: Glosses on the English Translation	Jacob Neusner
140056	Approaches to Modern Judaism II	Marc Lee Raphael
140057	Approaches to Judaism in Medieval Times II	David R. Blumenthal
140058	Midrash as Literature: The Primacy of Documentary Discourse	Jacob Neusner
140059	The Commerce of the Sacred: Mediation of the Divine Among Jews in the Graeco-Roman Diaspora	Jack N. Lightstone
140060	Major Trends in Formative Judaism I: Society and Symbol in Political Crisis	Jacob Neusner
140061	Major Trends in Formative Judaism II: Texts, Contents, and Contexts	Jacob Neusner
140062	A History of the Jews in Babylonia I: The Parthian Period	Jacob Neusner
140063	The Talmud of Babylonia: An American Translation XXXII: Tractate Arakhin	Jacob Neusner
140064	Ancient Judaism: Debates and Disputes	Jacob Neusner
140065	Prayers Alleged to Be Jewish: An Examination of the Constitutiones Apostolorum	David Fiensy
140066	The Legal Methodology of Hai Gaon	Tsvi Groner
140067	From Mishnah to Scripture: The Problem of the Unattributed Saying	Jacob Neusner
140068	Halakhah in a Theological Dimension	David Novak
140069	From Philo to Origen: Middle Platonism in Transition	Robert M. Berchman
140070	In Search of Talmudic Biography: The Problem of the Attributed Saying	Jacob Neusner
140071	The Death of the Old and the Birth of the New: The Framework of the Book of Numbers and the Pentateuch	Dennis T. Olson
140072	The Talmud of Babylonia: An American Translation XVII: Tractate Sotah	Jacob Neusner
140073	Understanding Seeking Faith: Essays on the Case of Judaism. Volume Two: Literature, Religion and the Social Study of Judiasm	Jacob Neusner
140074	The Talmud of Babylonia: An American Translation VI: Tractate Sukkah	Jacob Neusner

140075	Fear Not Warrior: A Study of 'al tira' Pericopes in the Hebrew Scriptures	Edgar W. Conrad
140076	Formative Judaism IV: Religious, Historical, and Literary Studies	Jacob Neusner
140077	Biblical Patterns in Modern Literature	Hirsch/Aschkenasy
140078	The Talmud of Babylonia: An American Translation I: Tractate Berakhot	Jacob Neusner
140079	Mishnah's Division of Agriculture: A History and Theology of Seder Zeraim	Alan J. Avery-Peck
140080	From Tradition to Imitation: The Plan and Program of Pesiqta Rabbati and Pesiqta deRab Kahana	Jacob Neusner
140081	The Talmud of Babylonia: An American Translation XXIIIA: Tractate Sanhedrin, Chapters 1-3	Jacob Neusner
140082	Jewish Presence in T. S. Eliot and Franz Kafka	Melvin Wilk
140083	School, Court, Public Administration: Judaism and its Institutions in Talmudic Babylonia	Jacob Neusner
140084	The Talmud of Babylonia: An American Translation XXIIIB: Tractate Sanhedrin, Chapters 4-8	Jacob Neusner
140085	The Bavli and Its Sources: The Question of Tradition in the Case of Tractate Sukkah	Jacob Neusner
140086	From Description to Conviction: Essays on the History and Theology of Judaism	Jacob Neusner
140087	The Talmud of Babylonia: An American Translation XXIIIC: Tractate Sanhedrin, Chapters 9-11	Jacob Neusner
140088	Mishnaic Law of Blessings and Prayers: Tractate Berakhot	Tzvee Zahavy
140089	The Peripatetic Saying: The Problem of the Thrice-Told Tale in Talmudic Literature	Jacob Neusner
140090	The Talmud of Babylonia: An American Translation XXVI: Tractate Horayot	Martin S. Jaffee
140091	Formative Judaism V: Religious, Historical, and Literary Studies	Jacob Neusner
140092	Essays on Biblical Method and Translation	Edward Greenstein
140093	The Integrity of Leviticus Rabbah	Jacob Neusner
140094	Behind the Essenes: History and Ideology of the Dead Sea Scrolls	Philip R. Davies
140095	Approaches to Judaism in Medieval Times, Volume III	David R. Blumenthal
140096	The Memorized Torah: The Mnemonic System of the Mishnah	Jacob Neusner
140097	Knowledge and Illumination	Hossein Ziai
140098	Sifre to Deuteronomy: An Analytical Translation Volume One: Pisqaot One through One Hundred Forty-Three. Debarim,Waethanan, Eqeb	Jacob Neusner
140099	Major Trends in Formative Judaism III: The Three Stages in the Formation of Judaism	Jacob Neusner
140101	Sifre to Deuteronomy: An Analytical Translation Volume Two: Pisqaot One Hundred Forty-Four through Three Hundred Fifty-Seven.Shofetim, Ki Tese, Ki Tabo, Nesabim, Ha'azinu, Zot Habberakhah	Jacob Neusner
140102	Sifra: The Rabbinic Commentary on Leviticus	Neusner/Brooks
140103	The Human Will in Judaism	Howard Eilberg-Schwartz
140104	Genesis Rabbah: Volume 1. Genesis 1:1 to 8:14	Jacob Neusner
140105	Genesis Rabbah: Volume 2. Genesis 8:15 to 28:9	Jacob Neusner
140106	Genesis Rabbah: Volume 3. Genesis 28:10 to 50:26	Jacob Neusner
140107	First Principles of Systemic Analysis	Jacob Neusner

140108	Genesis and Judaism	Jacob Neusner
140109	The Talmud of Babylonia: An American Translation XXXV: Tractates Meilah and Tamid	Peter J. Haas
140110	Studies in Islamic and Judaic Traditions	Brinner/Ricks
140111	Comparative Midrash: The Plan and Program of Genesis Rabbah and Leviticus Rabbah	Jacob Neusner
140112	The Tosefta: Its Structure and its Sources	Jacob Neusner
140113	Reading and Believing	Jacob Neusner
140114	The Fathers According to Rabbi Nathan	Jacob Neusner
140115	Etymology in Early Jewish Interpretation: The Hebrew Names in Philo	Lester L. Grabbe
140116	Understanding Seeking Faith: Essays on the Case of Judaism. Volume One: Debates on Method, Reports of Results	Jacob Neusner
140117	The Talmud of Babylonia.An American Translation VII: Tractate Besah	Alan J. Avery-Peck
140118	Sifre to Numbers: An American Translation and Explanation, Volume One: Sifre to Numbers 1-58	Jacob Neusner
140119	Sifre to Numbers: An American Translation and Explanation, Volume Two: Sifre to Numbers 59-115	Jacob Neusner
140120	Cohen and Troeltsch: Ethical Monotheistic Religion and Theory of Culture	Wendell S. Dietrich
140121	Goodenough on the History of Religion and on Judaism	Neusner/Frerichs
140122	Pesiqta deRab Kahana I: Pisqaot One through Fourteen	Jacob Neusner
140123	Pesiqta deRab Kahana II: Pisqaot Fifteen through Twenty-Eight and Introduction to Pesiqta deRab Kahana	Jacob Neusner
140124	Sifre to Deuteronomy: Introduction	Jacob Neusner
140126	A Conceptual Commentary on Midrash Leviticus Rabbah: Value Concepts in Jewish Thought	Max Kadushin
140127	The Other Judaisms of Late Antiquity	Alan F. Segal
140128	Josephus as a Historical Source in Patristic Literature through Eusebius	Michael Hardwick
140129	Judaism: The Evidence of the Mishnah	Jacob Neusner
140131	Philo, John and Paul: New Perspectives on Judaism and Early Christianity	Peder Borgen
140132	Babylonian Witchcraft Literature	Tzvi Abusch
140133	The Making of the Mind of Judaism: The Formative Age	Jacob Neusner
140135	Why No Gospels in Talmudic Judaism?	Jacob Neusner
140136	Torah: From Scroll to Symbol Part III: Doctrine	Jacob Neusner
140137	The Systemic Analysis of Judaism	Jacob Neusner
140138	Sifra: An Analytical Translation Vol. 1	Jacob Neusner
140139	Sifra: An Analytical Translation Vol. 2	Jacob Neusner
140140	Sifra: An Analytical Translation Vol. 3	Jacob Neusner
140141	Midrash in Context: Exegesis in Formative Judaism	Jacob Neusner
140143	Oxen, Women or Citizens? Slaves in the System of Mishnah	Paul V. Flesher
140144	The Book of the Pomegranate	Elliot R. Wolfson
140145	Wrong Ways and Right Ways in the Study of Formative Judaism	Jacob Neusner
140146	Sifra in Perspective: The Documentary Comparison of the Midrashim of Ancient Judaism	Jacob Neusner
140148	Mekhilta According to Rabbi Ishmael: An Analytical Translation Volume I	Jacob Neusner
140149	The Doctrine of the Divine Name: An Introduction to Classical Kabbalistic Theology	Stephen G. Wald
140150	Water into Wine and the Beheading of John the Baptist	Roger Aus

140151	The Formation of the Jewish Intellect	Jacob Neusner
140152	Mekhilta According to Rabbi Ishmael: An Introduction to Judaism's First Scriptural Encyclopaedia	Jacob Neusner
140153	Understanding Seeking Faith.Volume Three	Jacob Neusner
140154	Mekhilta According to Rabbi Ishmael: An Analytical Translation Volume Two	Jacob Neusner
140155	Goyim: Gentiles and Israelites in Mishnah-Tosefta	Gary P. Porton
140156	A Religion of Pots and Pans?	Jacob Neusner
140157	Claude Montefiore and Christianity	Maurice Gerald Bowler
140158	The Philosopical Mishnah Volume III	Jacob Neusner
140159	From Ancient Israel to Modern Judaism Volume 1: Intellect in Quest of Understanding	Neusner/Frerichs/Sarna
140160	The Social Study of Judaism Volume I	Jacob Neusner
140161	Philo's Jewish Identity	Alan Mendelson
140162	The Social Study of JudaismVolume II	Jacob Neusner
140163	The Philosophical Mishnah Volume I : The Initial Probe	Jacob Neusner
140164	The PhilosophicalMishnah Volume II : The Tractates Agenda: From Abodah Zarah Through Moed Qatan	Jacob Neusner
140166	Women's Earliest Records	Barbara S. Lesko
140167	The Legacy of Hermann Cohen	William Kluback
140168	Method and Meaning in Ancient Judaism	Jacob Neusner
140169	The Role of the Messenger and Message in the Ancient Near East	John T. Greene
140171	Abraham Heschel's Idea of Revelation	Lawerence Perlman
140172	The Philosophical Mishnah Volume IV: The Repertoire	Jacob Neusner
140173	From Ancient Israel to Modern Judaism Volume 2: Intellect in Quest of Understanding	Neusner/Frerichs/Sarna
140174	From Ancient Israel to Modern Judaism Volume 3: Intellect in Quest of Understanding	Neusner/Frerichs/Sarna
140175	From Ancient Israel to Modern Judaism Volume 4: Intellect in Quest of Understanding	Neusner/Frerichs/Sarna
140176	Translating the Classics of Judaism: In Theory and In Practice	Jacob Neusner
140177	Profiles of a Rabbi: Synoptic Opportunities in Reading About Jesus	Bruce Chilton
140178	Studies in Islamic and Judaic Traditions II	Brinner/Ricks
140179	Medium and Message in Judaism: First Series	Jacob Neusner
140180	Making the Classics of Judaism: The Three Stages of Literary Formation	Jacob Neusner
140181	The Law of Jealousy: Anthropology of Sotah	Adriana Destro
140182	Esther Rabbah I: An Analytical Translation	Jacob Neusner
140183	Ruth Rabbah: An Analytical Translation	Jacob Neusner
140184	Formative Judaism: Religious, Historical and Literary Studies	Jacob Neusner
140185	The Studia Philonica Annual 1989	David T. Runia
140186	The Setting of the Sermon on the Mount	W.D. Davies
140187	The Midrash Compilations of the Sixth and Seventh Centuries Volume One	Jacob Neusner
140188	The Midrash Compilations of the Sixth and Seventh Centuries Volume Two	Jacob Neusner
140189	The Midrash Compilations of the Sixth and Seventh Centuries Volume Three	Jacob Neusner
140190	The Midrash Compilations of the Sixth and Seventh Centuries Volume Four	Jacob Neusner

140191	The Religious World of Contemporary Judaism: Observations and Convictions	Jacob Neusner
140192	Approaches to Ancient Judaism: Volume VI	Neusner/Frerichs
140193	Lamentations Rabbah: An Analytical Translation	Jacob Neusner
140194	Early Christian Texts on Jews and Judaism	Robert S. MacLennan
140196	Torah and the Chronicler's History Work	Judson R. Shaver
140197	Song of Songs Rabbah: An Analytical Translation Volume One	Jacob Neusner
140198	Song of Songs Rabbah: An Analytical Translation Volume Two	Jacob Neusner
140199	From Literature to Theology in Formative Judaism	Jacob Neusner
140202	Maimonides on Perfection	Menachem Kellner
140203	The Martyr's Conviction	Eugene Weiner/Anita Weiner
140204	Judaism, Christianity, and Zoroastrianism in Talmudic Babylonia	Jacob Neusner
140205	Tzedakah: Can Jewish Philanthropy Buy Jewish Survival?	Jacob Neusner
140206	New Perspectives on Ancient Judaism: Volume 1	Neusner/Borgen Frerichs/Horsley
140207	Scriptures of the Oral Torah	Jacob Neusner
140208	Christian Faith and the Bible of Judaism	Jacob Neusner
140209	Philo's Perception of Women	Dorothy Sly
140210	Case Citation in the Babylonian Talmud: The Evidence Tractate Neziqin	Eliezer Segal
140211	The Biblical Herem: A Window on Israel's Religious Experience	Philip D. Stern
140212	Goodenough on the Beginnings of Christianity	A.T. Kraabel
140213	The Talmud of Babylonia: An American Translation XXIA: Tractate Bava Mesia Chapters 1-2	Jacob Neusner
140214	The Talmud of Babylonia: An American Translation XXIB: Tractate Bava Mesia Chapters 3-4	Jacob Neusner
140215	The Talmud of Babylonia: An American Translation XXIC: Tractate Bava Mesia Chapters 5-6	Jacob Neusner
140216	The Talmud of Babylonia: An American Translation XXID: Tractate Bava Mesia Chapters 7-10	Jacob Neusner
140217	Semites, Iranians, Greeks and Romans: Studies in their Interactions	Jonathan A. Goldstein
140218	The Talmud of Babylonia: An American Translation XXXIII: Temurah	Jacob Neusner
140219	The Talmud of Babylonia: An American Translation XXXIA: Tractate Bekhorot Chapters 1-4	Jacob Neusner
140220	The Talmud of Babylonia: An American Translation XXXIB: Tractate Bekhorot Chapters 5-9	Jacob Neusner
140221	The Talmud of Babylonia: An American Translation XXXVIA: Tractate Niddah Chapters 1-3	Jacob Neusner
140222	The Talmud of Babylonia: An American Translation XXXVIB: Tractate Niddah Chapters 4-10	Jacob Neusner
140223	The Talmud of Babylonia: An American Translation XXXIV: Tractate Keritot	Jacob Neusner
140224	Paul, the Temple, and the Presence of God	David A. Renwick
140225	The Book of the People	William W. Hallo
140226	The Studia Philonica Annual 1990	David Runia
140227	The Talmud of Babylonia: An American Translation XXVA: Tractate Abodah Zarah Chapters 1-2	Jacob Neusner
140228	The Talmud of Babylonia: An American Translation XXVB: Tractate Abodah Zarah Chapters 3-5	Jacob Neusner
140230	The Studia Philonica Annual 1991	David Runia

140231	The Talmud of Babylonia: An American Translation XXVIIIA: Tractate Zebahim Chapters 1-3	Jacob Neusner
140232	Both Literal and Allegorical: Studies in Philo of Alexandria's Questions and Answers on Genesis and Exodus	David M. Hay
140233	The Talmud of Babylonia: An American Translation XXVIIIB: Tractate Zebahim Chapters 4-8	Jacob Neusner
140234	The Talmud of Babylonia: An American Translation XXVIIIC: Tractate Zebahim Chapters 9-14	Jacob Neusner
140235	The Talmud of Babylonia: An American Translation XXIXA: Tractate Menahot Chapters 1-3	Jacob Neusner
140236	The Talmud of Babylonia: An American Translation XXIXB: Tractate Menahot Chapters 4-7	Jacob Neusner
140237	The Talmud of Babylonia: An American Translation XXIXC: Tractate Menahot Chapters 8-13	Jacob Neusner
140238	The Talmud of Babylonia: An American Translation XXIX: Tractate Makkot	Jacob Neusner
140239	The Talmud of Babylonia: An American Translation XXIIA: Tractate Baba Batra Chapters 1-2	Jacob Neusner
140240	The Talmud of Babylonia: An American Translation XXIIB: Tractate Baba Batra Chapter 3	Jacob Neusner
140241	The Talmud of Babylonia: An American Translation XXIIC: Tractate Baba Batra Chapters 4-6	Jacob Neusner
140242	The Talmud of Babylonia: An American Translation XXVIIA: Tractate Shebuot	Jacob Neusner
140243	The Talmud of Babylonia: An American Translation XXVIIB: Tractate Shebuot	Jacob Neusner
140244	Balaam and His Interpreters: A Hermeneutical History of the Balaam Traditions	John T. Greene
140245	Courageous Universality: The Work of Schmuel Hugo Bergman	William Kluback
140246	The Mechanics of Change: Essays in the Social History of German Jewry	Steven M. Lowenstein
140247	The Talmud of Babylonia: An American Translation XXA: Tractate Baba Qamma Chapters 1-3	Jacob Neusner
140248	The Talmud of Babylonia: An American Translation XXB : Tractate Baba Qamma Chapters 4-7	Jacob Neusner
140249	The Talmud of Babylonia: An American Translation XXC: Tractate Baba Qamma Chapters 8-10	Jacob Neusner
140250	The Talmud of Babylonia: An American Translation XIIIA: Tractate Yebamot Chapters 1-3	Jacob Neusner
140251	The Talmud of Babylonia: An American Translation XIIIB: Tractate Yebamot Chapters 4-6	Jacob Neusner
140252	The Talmud of Babylonia: An American Translation XI: Tractate Moed Qatan	Jacob Neusner
140253	The Talmud of Babylonia: An American Translation XXX.A: Tractate Hullin	Tzvee Zahavy
140254	The Talmud of Babylonia: An American Translation XXX.B: Tractate Hullin	Tzvee Zahavy
140255	The Talmud of Babylonia: An American Translation XXX.C: Tractate Hullin	Tzvee Zahavy
140256	The Talmud of Babylonia: An American Translation XIII.C: Tractate Yebamot	Jacob Neusner
140257	The Talmud of Babylonia: An American Translation XIV.A: Tractate Ketubot	Jacob Neusner

140258	*The Talmud of Babylonia: An American Translation XIV.B: Tractate Ketubot*	Jacob Neusner
140260	*The Talmud of Babylonia: An American Translation XIV.C: Tractate Ketubot*	Jacob Neusner
140261	*The Talmud of Babylonia: An American Translation XIII.D: Tractate Yebamot*	Jacob Neusner

Brown Studies on Jews and Their Societies

145001	*American Jewish Fertility*	Calvin Goldscheider
145003	*The American Jewish Community*	Calvin Goldscheider
145004	*The Naturalized Jews of the Grand Duchy of Posen in 1834 and 1835*	Edward David Luft
145005	*Suburban Communities: The Jewishness of American Reform Jews*	Gerald L. Showstack
145007	*Ethnic Survival in America*	David Schoem
145008	*American Jews in the 21st Century: A Leadership Challenge*	Earl Raab

Brown Studies in Religion

147001	*Religious Writings and Religious Systems Volume 1*	Jacob Neusner, et al
147002	*Religious Writings and Religious Systems Volume 2*	Jacob Neusner, et al
147003	*Religion and the Social Sciences*	Robert Segal